PRACTICE
— OF —
FEELING GOOD

HOW TO UPGRADE YOUR
THINKING AND LIVE A
FEEL-GOOD LIFE

FLETCHER ELLINGSON

Copyright © 2023 by Fletcher Ellingson

All rights reserved. No part of this publication may be reproduced, distributed, or transmitted in any form or by any means without prior written permission.

Fletcher Ellingson -- 1st ed.
Chief Editor, Shannon Buritz

ISBN: 978-1-954757-39-4

The Publisher has strived to be as accurate and complete as possible in the creation of this book.

This book is not intended for use as a legal, business, accounting, or financial advice source. All readers are advised to seek the services of competent professionals in legal, business, accounting, and finance fields.

Like anything else in life, there are no guarantees of income or results in practical advice books. Readers are cautioned to rely on their judgment about their individual circumstances to act accordingly.

While all attempts have been made to verify information provided in this publication, the Publisher assumes no responsibility for errors, omissions, or contrary interpretation of the subject matter herein. Any perceived slights of specific persons, peoples, or organizations are unintentional.

I dedicate this book to my wife and partner in life, Amy. Thank you for believing in me, seeing and accepting me for who I am, and being a constant source of inspiration and encouragement to become the next version of myself.

CONTENTS

Foreword by David Bayer — vii
Introduction — xi
How to Read This Book — xvii

Chapter 1 Can I Really Rewire My Brain? — 1
Chapter 2 What You Focus On, You Feel — 17
Chapter 3 Suffering vs. Feeling Good — 27
Chapter 4 The Gift in Fear — 43
Chapter 5 The Practice of Overcoming an Upset — 57
Chapter 6 Your Values Don't Mean Jack — 75
Chapter 7 Gratitude — 89
Chapter 8 How to Transform Resentment — 97
Chapter 9 Life's Magic Wand — 111
Chapter 10 Putting It All Into Practice — 121

Acknowledgments — 135
About Fletcher Ellingson — 137
What Fletcher's Clients Are Saying… — 139

FOREWORD

If you were to look behind all of your efforts to make more money, get clarity on your purpose, find your soulmate, create extraordinary relationships, take on your health and fitness, be supportive and kind parents, or contribute to society in a meaningful way– it would all boil down to one thing: Your desire to feel good.

But what if you didn't need to achieve your goals, be successful, or desperately attempt to control your external circumstances in order to be happy? What if, just maybe, by learning how to feel good now, you could achieve your vision for your life and, more importantly, be happy regardless?

When I first met Fletcher, he had already been in one of my programs for nearly a year. I realized at that time that I had barely noticed him. That's actually a compliment – a big one. He was one of about a hundred goal-achieving, personal development-loving, growth-seeking entrepreneurs in one of my high-level coaching programs. But he didn't stand out. Not because he isn't remarkable as a person (because he is) but because his process was internal. While some members of our group publicly shared their breakthroughs, opinions, and observations – and others needed higher or greater levels of hands-on coaching or support – Fletcher had his own unique way of playing full out. He was one hundred percent committed to the inner work. He was humble, and he was focused.

Fletcher is different, and therefore, so is this book. Every once in a while, you meet someone so focused on their process that they don't really stand out – until they break out. Over four years in my community, and for decades prior, Fletcher has been obsessed not about how to achieve his goals or make more money (although that's the byproduct) or how to become successful or well known. He's been focused on the nucleus that really matters – how to feel good. And he's mastered it.

Look, there's a lot of material out there on motivation, self-help, spiritual growth, personal growth, mindset, emotional intelligence, and high performance – and that's a good thing. If you want to create change in the way you think and the way you feel, it's necessary to approach the topic from a multitude of perspectives. It's what allows you to develop personal mastery. But all those books and topics are leading you to the one thing that Fletcher has studied, scrutinized, tested, integrated, and become phenomenal at: the practice of feeling good. And that's precisely what it is – a practice.

If you want to learn how to change your brain to be less reactive and more responsive to the increasingly dynamic circumstances of your life, you must have both the teachings and the tools and, most importantly, commit to a daily living practice. This book was created with the intention of giving you everything you need to feel good *now*. Fletcher doesn't leave you with airy-fairy euphemisms of positive psychology or hopeful thinking. He gives you a map for the one and only thing that leads to all transformation – a change in your brain and the way you think.

Each section of this book contains valuable teachings, takeaways, and an invitation to try on everything that Fletcher shares with you. This book and its contents are not based on intellectual understanding but road-tested experience by someone who has experienced the entire range of triumphs, challenges, highs, and lows and used those experiences as a catalyst for massive personal growth.

As you trust his process, you'll find deeper levels of self-awareness, a significant reduction in your stress, anxiety, and overwhelm, and the ability to achieve more, if not all, your goals. But ultimately, what this book creates is a real possibility of achieving more of the one thing we all truly want. To feel good.

- David Bayer
Visionary, Philosopher, Teacher, and CEO of David Bayer Evolutionary Technologies

INTRODUCTION

When was the last time you intentionally upgraded your thinking? We upgrade our phones, laptops, and cars, but what about upgrading our thoughts, beliefs, and attitudes? When was the last time you upgraded the operating system in your head to make decisions more effectively and listen, speak, create, and express yourself at a higher level? Have you ever thought, "Today, I'm going to begin creating new neural pathways in my brain, which will provide access to new thinking, take new actions, and, in turn, yield new results?" Chances are you may never have thought about this. The very concept that we can upgrade our thinking like a software program may seem odd, improbable, and inaccessible. After all, why would we think such a thing? It isn't a concept taught in schools or a hot topic we discuss socially.

Technology companies are in a never-ending race to upgrade all of our watches, phones, computers, TVs, cars, and now AI. They are constantly working on ways to improve and expand our ability to communicate, manage data, and create art, to name just a few examples. So why don't we put as much consideration into upgrading our thinking? Everything initiates with our thoughts, including love, war, peace, jealousy, trust, art, marriage, divorce, etcetera. Doesn't it make sense to make upgrades to the very thing that determines our entire experience of life?

It makes a lot of sense to me, and I have the privilege of witnessing the amazing outcomes that occur in my clients' lives after they change their thinking. My line of work involves helping people radically change their thinking to produce new outcomes in their health, wealth, and relationships. I feel grateful and fortunate that I am able to interact with so many interesting people in my career. Among my clients are police officers, massage therapists, stay-at-home parents, physicians, real estate professionals, attorneys, managers, veterinarians, teachers, CEOs, and a broad spectrum of entrepreneurs. As you can see, my clients are varied. And yet what I've come to discover is that no matter what their career is, their relationship status, their race, their sexual orientation, or what their bank account balance is, they all have one thing in common: they all want to feel good in life. They want to feel good about their health, wealth, and relationships. And, often, they have great ideas about what they should do to feel good. But, things like fear, resistance, self-doubt, disappointments, insecurity, and upsets continue to get in the way of experiencing a feel-good life as frequently and intensely as they desire. Many of them report that feeling "bad" or a sense of suffering is highly prevalent in their daily lives.

Now, humans are an intelligent species. So why do we spend so much time worried, stressed, fearful, and insecure? Why is it so challenging to have a feel-good life? Some would argue it's a lack of knowledge or education. That could be part of it but only a minor part. All of my clients have a lot of knowledge, which, if implemented, could make a massive difference in their lives. However, in certain areas of life, they find themselves simply unable to implement it or to maintain effective actions. They don't understand why they can't get themselves to do what they know they should be doing. So you see, knowledge is not enough. Positive thinking is not enough. This is not a book about positive thinking. It's a book about reprogramming, upgrading, and evolving our thinking to create an extraordinary, consistent, feel-good living experience.

We will spend much time discussing "feeling good" in the following pages. So let me define what I mean when I use that phrase. Feeling good is a state of mind encompassing one or more of the following in the illustration below.

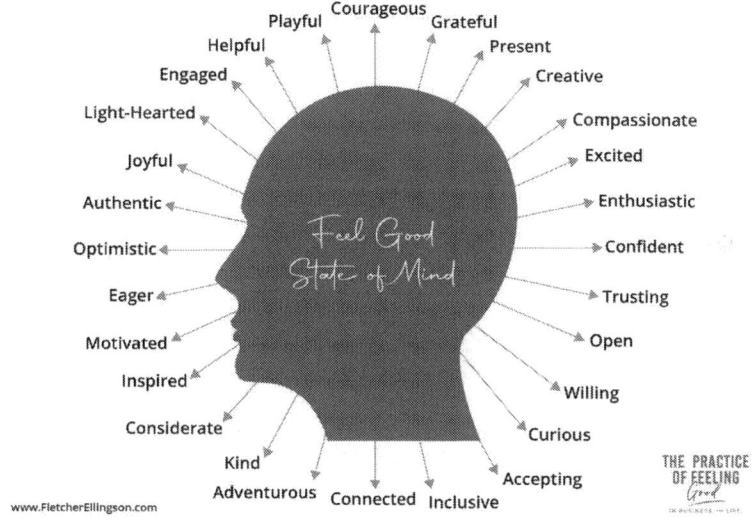

If we were experiencing life with many of the descriptors displayed in the above graphic more regularly and consistently, wouldn't life feel incredible? We would feel like we're on top of the world and that anything is possible. But the fact is that feeling like this is rare for many people, if not most. I work with talented, capable, intelligent, and successful people. And still, what they frequently report is a noticeable lack of feeling good. They experience a lot of mental suffering in the form of worry, stress, overwhelm, loneliness, fear, frustration, anger, insecurity, jealousy, confusion, uncertainty, and anxiety. I want to be clear about something here. There's nothing wrong with any of our feelings or emotions. And there's nothing right about them either. In this book, we shift the conversation away from specific emotional states and courses of action as being morally good, bad, right, or wrong. Instead, we want to practice asking, "Is this serving my life?" The opportunity is to realize that every emotion has a message for us. Let's become curious about the message.

I'll give you a couple of examples. Sometimes we feel guilty. Guilt is not inherently a bad emotion; in fact, it has a very important message to which we should pay attention. When you experience guilt, the message is that you violated one of your own personal rules or morals or one of the rules of the community. That community could be a marriage, a family, an organization, or a local or global community. It has everything to do with an action you've taken (or not taken) that violates a rule, code, or ethic. Contrast that feeling with shame. What's the message of shame? The message of shame has nothing to do with our actions. It has everything to do with who we believe we are. And it's usually a sense that there's something deficient, lacking, or broken about us. It's a sense of not being good enough. What about frustration? The message of frustration is that something is not happening the way we want it to. The message of worry is that we're not trusting and not in the present moment. It's helpful to pay attention to the message of our emotions. They can help us better understand our thinking, beliefs, and decision-making.

Again, this is not about right or wrong. I used to be highly judgmental about other people and myself. I divided people into right, wrong, good, bad, fair, and unfair. And the cost of living like that was frequent mental suffering. It held me back tremendously in my ability to create a feel-good life. In a sense, I was poisoning my own well. I became practiced at the game of noticing, labeling, and dividing people's actions and themselves into categories. It is a tiresome and divisive way to go through life. It held me back in my finances, relationships, and my health.

But then I began to change my thinking, to upgrade it intentionally. My logic said if my thinking were different, my questions would be different, my actions would be different, and therefore, my results would have to be different. My financial trajectory dramatically changed when I began to replace old ways of thinking and behaviors with new ones. I went from living paycheck to paycheck to having a savings account that actually had money in it. I began investing in real estate and the stock market and learning a few fundamentals about creating wealth. My health and fitness transformed. I went from never caring about what I ate and rarely exercising to fueling my body with a better diet and completing several triathlons. The chronic joint pain throughout my body that I had been dealing with for years cleared up. And it allowed me to create a marriage beyond what I had ever dreamed was possible.

When we feel good in life, we have access to powerfully creating an extraordinary living experience. However, there is one big catch - feeling good takes practice and a lot of it. But it is worth it! So if you're ready for a practice that I've seen mend families, build businesses, kick addictions, construct loving relationships, and create health, I have an invitation for you. I invite you to join me in the practice of feeling good.

- Fletcher Ellingson

HOW TO READ THIS BOOK

This book was created largely from the content of one of my coaching courses called "The Practice of Feeling Good." I will introduce you to several of the key concepts that can provide access to creating new and desired outcomes in your life. My intention is that the book is read in the order the chapters are written. The concepts and distinctions build on each other, and by the end, you will have a toolbox that will help you navigate life with greater ease and create more feel-good moments.

1

CAN I REALLY REWIRE MY BRAIN?

Our nervous system, including our brain, has systems or what I call "programs" to regulate every area of our lives. And these programs were created without our permission and usually without our awareness. It is important to examine and seek to have at least a basic understanding of your programs because they determine your thoughts, actions, outcomes, and, therefore, your destiny. If we go through life ignorant of these programs, we are at a serious disadvantage when it comes to creating a fulfilling life. But, if we practice the process of self-inquiry, we have access to creating new programs. As George Lucas said, "We are all living in cages with the door wide open." We just need to understand what makes up our cage and where the door is.

You've heard the expression that you can't teach an old dog new tricks. Well, if you have ever watched Cesar Milan work, you know that any dog can learn new things. Cesar is skilled at working with dogs with histories of abuse, neglect, abandonment, anxiety, and persistent problematic behaviors. The ages of the dogs are irrelevant. He works with young, middle-aged, and older dogs. How does he have such great success when others do not? The secret is that Caesar understands the programming of dogs. Caesar doesn't get a dog to stop a particular behavior. He doesn't get them to stop barking, biting, or jumping up on people. Instead, he teaches the dog to begin a *new behavior*. He teaches them, first and foremost, to pay attention to him, connect with him, and be present with him. He then teaches them to sit, wait, lie down, and come when called. The dog transitions from anxious and stressed to calm and secure. It's an amazing thing to watch, and it actually doesn't take that long. Look him up on YouTube if you have not seen him work his magic. It is an excellent illustration of how quickly new behaviors can be created and maintained with the right training and support structure.

At the core of what Cesar does is to help the dog's brain create new programming and rewire the nervous system, which allows for a new and more desired outcome. This is very similar to the work we do in The Practice of Feeling Good. We are not trying to get you to stop behaviors; we are inviting you to step into a practice of new thinking and new behaviors. We are attempting to rewire parts of the brain and nervous system. Consider that all we are is the sum of our programming. We have programs that run our thinking around health, fitness, finances, and relationships. We have programs around what we deem is good, bad, right, or wrong. These programs constantly run without our permission, consent, or approval. They are the filters through which we view life and therefore determine our destiny.

I want to emphasize that last thought: **Our programming determines our destiny.** Some may read that and think, "Come on, Fletcher, that's a bit dramatic." I get why people might think that. Especially in a culture where a popular belief is that you can be whoever you want, do whatever you want, and have whatever you want, particularly if you work hard in life. I agree with that to an extent; however, I would modify it to say that you can be, do, or have whatever you want, but only if it aligns with your programming. The outcomes we have in life are always in alignment with our programming. Our programming can keep us caged, or it can set us free. To understand this, I'll give you a 30,000-foot overview of what I mean by "programming."

PROGRAMMING FUNDAMENTALS

Our programs are cybernetic loops. What is a cybernetic loop? It's a type of self-regulating system. A simple example of a self-regulating system is a home's thermostat. You program the system to warm the house when it gets too cold and to cool the house when it gets too hot. Once the system is set, it regulates the temperature by itself and produces the desired outcome. It does it without you having to be involved. Our bodies have all sorts of self-regulating systems which control everything, including our temperature, breathing, blood circulation, the release of hormones, digestion, self-protection behaviors, and procreation, to name a few. All of these regulating systems operate on their own. They don't require us to turn them on or off. They are designed to run without our involvement. You can interrupt some of them if you are intentional. For instance, you can hold your breath or intentionally slow your heartbeat, but only temporarily. After a short time, the program will take over. Your body will not let you hold your breath to the point of dying.

The cybernetic loops in our brain regarding health, wealth, and relationships are similar, though they also have some distinct differences. Think of these loops as "loops of causality." Look at what I call the "Cycle of Six" below.

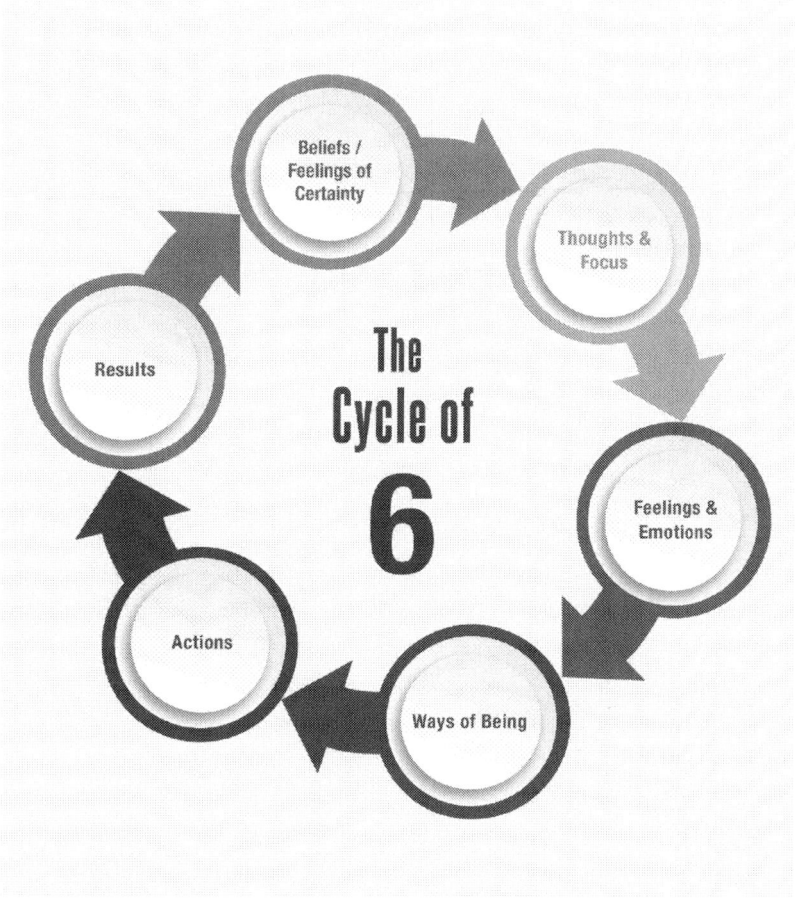

We did not intentionally or even knowingly create most of our programs. Did anyone ask what you wanted to believe about money, marriage, education, justice, or sex? How about who you can or cannot trust? No. You were simply told and shown at a young age by family members, teachers, church, government, friends, and media. The programming began the moment you entered the world. It started without your consent or knowledge of it. Let's look at an example.

When Angela was six years old, she was bitten by a medium-sized dog. Before this incident, Angela loved dogs and wanted to pet them and play with them whenever she saw them. However, for many years after the dog bite incident, she was highly fearful of all dogs, no matter their size. She would avoid dogs in the neighborhood, even going to the extreme of crossing the street if she saw one off-leash. If Angela went to a friend's house with a dog, it would need to be locked up in a room or outside. She was unwilling to risk an encounter with a dog because her program about them constantly reminded her that dogs were dangerous and could not be trusted. To ensure she paid attention, the program automatically conjured up fearful memories of the past incident when she was six. Her brain would present her with images of worst-case scenarios. And because the brain must create an emotion (also known as a chemical reaction) that aligns with the thoughts Angela was focused on, she would feel a rush of fear and adrenaline. This caused Angela to resist visiting homes or parks where dogs would be present. If a dog looked her way or attempted to approach or sniff her, she immediately pulled back and became defensive. Her ways of being around dogs became insecure and fearful.

Our "ways of being" determine the actions we take. So Angela would pass on going to sleepovers at friends' homes with dogs and missed out on several birthday parties and celebrations. Eventually, some of her friends just stopped asking her to come over. Not getting invited felt terrible to her. She became even more insecure and now resentful of some of her friends. It wouldn't be until Angela was almost 30 years old that she would realize the decision she had made when she was six. She had no idea that a decision made by a six-year-old in the blink of an eye would become a full-blown program, a cybernetic loop that would create thoughts, emotions, and a way of being which would determine her actions and produce results that would ultimately reinforce and strengthen the program.

This is what I call the "Cycle of Six." It is the loop of causality. Our programs run our lives. If you have ever made decisions you knew were not aligned with your morals and ethics, it's because your programming was activated and overrode those morals and ethics. Sometimes we lie or cheat or blow up in an argument. Even though it goes against our morals, it just seems to happen. But it happened because our programming was activated. And we didn't realize it, or we did realize it but didn't understand how to interrupt it.

We have programs that serve us well. And others that hold us back and can make a huge mess of our lives. Your programs will run you and determine the quality of life and your actual destiny. For many of us, that destiny will not be the feel-good destiny we dreamed of in our youth. And unless we can identify the programs and learn to set up new ones, we end up modeling and passing these same programs on to our children. While we tell them they can do anything and be anything, our actions and much of what they hear us say really conveys, "Life is a struggle. Money doesn't grow on trees. Play it safe. Don't take big risks. Follow the pack. There's never enough time. Be reasonable."

At this point, you may ask, "What can I do about the programs holding me back and not serving me?" That is an excellent critical question. Let's take a look at a straightforward methodology to answer this question. I've had the wonderful opportunity to study with outstanding coaches and mentors in my life. The following methodology, which has been extremely helpful to my clients and me, came from spending time with people I consider giants in the personal evolution conversation. Thank you, Tony Robbins, Esther Hicks, David Bayer, Louise Hay, and Bob Proctor, to name just a few. My four years studying with David Bayer and the legendary tribe helped me understand this framework at a much deeper level.

STEP ONE: IDENTIFY THE PROGRAM

We can identify the program by asking more critical questions. We start by addressing the top circle in the Cycle of Six diagram, which contains your beliefs or feelings of certainty. A helpful way of being in life is to be curious. For example, ask yourself, "What do I believe about money?" Listen for the answer. It may be one of the following: "Money is hard to generate. I never have enough money. Money slips through my fingers. Money is evil. Money causes problems. I'm not good with money." Whatever the answer is, it's an insight into the program. What you believe will determine which thoughts the mind generates. You may assume that you think these thoughts, but **you** don't. It is your program that generates the automatic thoughts about money. Notice that you have had these thoughts many times before. In fact, they're frequently the same thoughts and are very familiar. That's because they are habitual thoughts. It's easy for the mind to generate them because they are part of an often-run program with deep grooves.

STEP TWO: DOES THE BELIEF OR THOUGHT SERVE YOUR LIFE?

If yes, then great. Focus on the thought and similar ones even more. Focus on them with intention because what you focus on, you feel. What you focus on expands, and what you focus on becomes your point of attraction. This is an important part of the practice of feeling good. However, if the answer is no, this thought does not feel good and doesn't serve my life, then we're going to do something radical.

STEP THREE: DECLARE THAT THE BELIEF IS INACCURATE

I know it sounds counterintuitive but stay with me. The methodology works, and it's how you interrupt the program. We declare that the belief is inaccurate. Remember Angela, who had decided that dogs were dangerous and couldn't be trusted? She had to declare her belief was inaccurate even though this declaration didn't feel comfortable or real to her.

STEP FOUR: DECLARE THAT SOME FORM OF THE OPPOSITE OF THE BELIEF IS ACCURATE

Again, in Angela's case, she believed that dogs were dangerous and could not be trusted. That belief didn't feel good emotionally, and it didn't serve her life. So she assumed it must not be accurate. Then she had to declare that some form of the opposite of that belief must be accurate. So she came up with the following: "Most dogs are friendly and safe." Whoa, what a departure from her previous belief!

Now, the above four steps will not eliminate the program; they only serve to interrupt and slow it down. It's an opportunity to see the program and begin operating outside it. It's the beginning of creating freedom from the existing program. Remember earlier when I stated that Cesar Milan was not teaching the dogs how to stop a bad behavior? He was teaching the dogs a new behavior and having them focus on that. Similarly, we can't eliminate our old programming; however, we can teach our brains to use a new program which we set up intentionally. In many cases, the old programming will still be in there; it can still get activated. The difference is we don't get stuck in the old programming for as long, the intensity is diminished, and the frequency of the program being triggered is lessened.

But this is key. Unless there is another program for the brain to use, it will have no choice but to use the old program. We must set up a new program for the brain to use. This is what can alter our destiny. New programming causes new thoughts, which causes new emotions, which causes new ways of being, which then causes new actions. And those new actions produce new outcomes which ultimately reinforce the new program.

Now, this is where things get very interesting and very exciting. Step four does not create a new program by itself. In step four, you have simply identified a new belief you want but do not yet have. So how do we get this new belief to stick? Let's take a look at the next step.

STEP FIVE: GATHER MASSIVE EVIDENCE

When attorneys prepare to argue in court, they gather massive amounts of evidence to create a compelling case. They want to create a significant sense of certainty in the mind of the judge and jury. The person who wins is the one with the most convincing evidence-based story. This is how our brain works too. Our brain is constantly gathering evidence to support our beliefs. It's how beliefs become stronger and stronger. Once you decide that dogs are dangerous, your mind pays attention to anything in the physical world that you hear, read about, or see that will support the notion that dogs are dangerous. If a dog barks at you, if you hear of someone who was bitten, if a dog looks your way, the brain files it away as evidence in the "dogs are dangerous" file.

Eventually, you amass an extensive file of evidence for your brain to reference about dogs and surprise, it all points to the fact that dogs are out to get you and cannot be trusted. This is how all of your beliefs were set up. Without you knowing, your mind began to pay attention to and collect massive amounts of evidence to support your beliefs, not caring whether or not the belief was accurate. You see, the brain isn't interested in true, false, right, or wrong. **It simply must gather evidence in support of the belief because you decided it was so.**

So Angela began gathering evidence to make a winning case. She started watching videos of puppies playing and noticed how cute they looked. Then she began watching videos of well-trained dogs, seeing eye dogs, and other service dogs that helped people with medical conditions. She watched videos of dogs playing with toddlers and witnessed how gentle they could be. She even saw funny videos of dogs playing with other types of animals. When Angela watched these images, she would repeat her new desired belief: "Most dogs are friendly and safe." Eventually, she decided to meet some newborn yellow lab puppies. She knew these pups couldn't hurt her, as they could barely navigate their surroundings. Angela picked them up, felt their softness, heard their little puppy whines, and she found herself smiling and laughing at them as they scooted and tumbled around on the floor. She reminded herself that most dogs were friendly and safe. This was certainly the case with this little pack of pups. She visited the puppies a handful of times over the next few weeks and was surprised by how easy it was to be with them and that she even enjoyed it.

During that experience, Angela also learned how to sit with the mama dog as the pups were nursing. She witnessed how the mother dog was non-threatening and nurturing. Angela was able to pet the mama dog, connect with her, and feel safe. This was a significant breakthrough for her. The new program was taking hold.

STEP SIX: DETERMINE YOUR WAY OF BEING

Angela did one other extremely important thing. She chose her ways of being. She chose to be open, willing, courageous, and, most importantly, trusting. These ways of being gave her access to taking new actions.

This step is critical. Along with our thoughts, our ways of being influence our actions. Consider it. If your way of being is fearful, you will likely fight, flee, or freeze. You take actions that are in alignment with your way of being. Furthermore, our ways of being can become habitual and then become a character trait. They become a permanent part of who you are. Have you ever met someone who generally seems "closed off" or "cynical?" Maybe you know people who seem "easygoing" or "open" to life. They have practiced these ways of being for so long that they become part of who they are, influencing their actions and the results they experience.

Consider which ways of being will serve your life in a particular setting. For example, if you want to create peace in a relationship experiencing a lot of upset but your ways of being are judgemental, defensive, and closed, it will be challenging to arrive at peace. However, if your ways of being are present, curious, accepting, open, and willing, you have access to creating peace in that relationship.

When Angela combined her new ways of being with all the new evidence she had collected, it became impossible to return to her old belief. This transformation occurred as a result of deliberately programming the mind.

To help you identify empowering ways of being, I have included what I refer to as the "Chart of Feel Good Elements." I find it useful when I want to intentionally move the needle in an area of my life. I encourage you to identify three or four elements and make your own Feel Good Compound. One of my favorite compounds is Resourceful, Capable, and Flexible. I love this compound. For me, being resourceful, capable, and flexible is my access point to being able to create my life powerfully. That feels good! Have fun with this chart. What feel good compounds would be helpful for your marriage or parenting, your health and fitness, or your financial life? I would love to hear what compounds you come up with and for which areas of your life. Shoot me an email and share your inspiration.

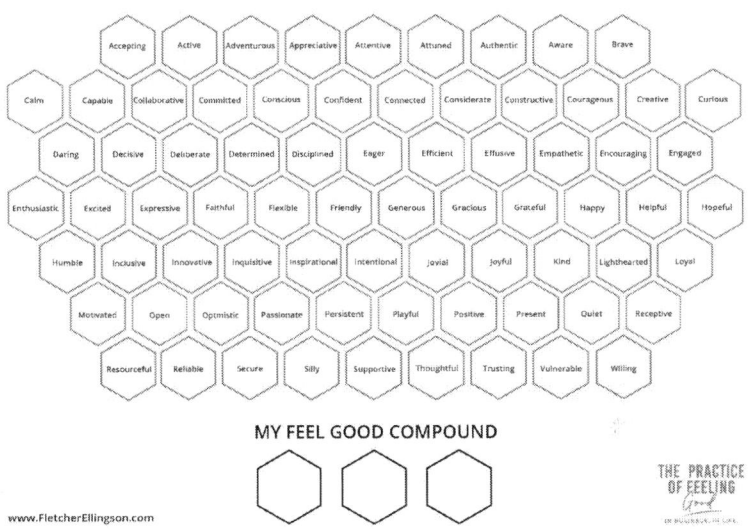

Key Takeaways

- Almost all of our programs were created without our knowledge or consent.

- We can interrupt programs temporarily. But unless there is a new program, the brain will continue to use the existing one even if it doesn't serve our life.

- We have the ability to intentionally set up new beliefs in any area of our life using a simple 6-step methodology.

Opportunity to Practice

Practice getting curious. Write down the answers you hear your mind say when you ask the following questions:

- What do I believe about money?
- What thoughts, memories, or images does this question cause my mind to think?
- What emotions do I feel as a result of these thoughts?
- What ways of being do I notice? Example: Frugal, judgemental, generous, cynical, resigned, optimistic, responsible, eager, daring
- What actions do I take or not take due to these beliefs and emotions?
- What are the results of the actions I took or did not take?
- Has this belief served me or held me back? It could be a bit of both.
- Is it time to create a new belief? Go for it!

Now do the same exercise for the following questions:

- What do I believe about my intelligence?

- What do I believe about my health and fitness?

- What do I believe about people?

- What do I believe about my career?

- What do I believe about myself? Am I enough? Do I have what it takes?

These are just a few questions to get you going. You can do this in any area of your life. Get curious about what you believe, and it will illuminate the programs that have been operating in your life.

2

WHAT YOU FOCUS ON, YOU FEEL

"Hey Fletcher, what do you know for sure?" This was how one of my good friends greeted me as we met to play pickleball. It's an excellent question to consider, "What do I know for sure?" With each year that passes and the more I experience, it becomes increasingly clear that there is very little I know "for sure." So I answered with one of the few things I feel absolutely certain about, "What you focus on, you feel." I believe this one statement has profound implications on the quality of every moment of our lives.

The brain's ability to distinguish between what is real and what is not real is minimal. In this chapter, I'll demonstrate this concept and why becoming familiar with it is critical to creating more "feeling good" in our lives.

NOTHING MORE THAN A SILVER SCREEN

Imagine a new movie is coming to your local theater that you've been waiting several months to see. You've seen previews that promise a movie filled with excitement, drama, comedy, romance, and unexpected twists and turns. Picture yourself paying for the tickets at the box office with a friend, grabbing your favorite snacks, and finding a seat. All around you, seats are filling up, and there are sounds of muffled conversations and rustling candy wrappers. As the lights go down, the movie begins, almost immediately pulling you to the edge of your seat as you are captivated by the opening action sequence. You're not eating your popcorn because you're fixated on what's happening on the screen. In fact, if someone were to monitor your vitals, it would easily show an increased heart rate.

After several minutes, the action scene ends. You take a deep breath and let out a big exhalation as you realize you have been holding your breath during the high-intensity action. Now you adjust your body and relax back into your seat. The scene changes to something more comedic, and you laugh aloud with the rest of the audience. Another 30 minutes in, a heart-wrenching tragedy strikes involving the main character, and your eyes well up with tears. You look over at your friend, who has tears streaming down their face. But it only takes another 15 minutes to turn those tears into belly laughs again. And another 15 to widen your eyes at another compelling action scene. This time, one of the main characters displays incredible courage in the face of fear and opposition. As a result of that courage, the protagonist overcomes a huge obstacle and experiences an exhilarating victory. You feel moved and inspired as the music swells. Audience members begin to applaud and cheer for the hero. Finally, the movie wraps up with a good dose of heartfelt resolution, and the final scene of levity puts a smile on everyone's face. The credits roll, and the house lights begin to come up.

We've all been through this situation, but what really just

happened? A two-hour roller coaster ride of very real and intense emotions happened. You laughed, cried, and gasped. You experienced surprise, thrill, and delight. You likely went through a broader range of emotions than you do in an entire day or even a week.

How is this possible? It's possible because your mind responds to something presented to you on a screen in the same way it responds to actual events in your life. While in the theater, your mind reacts emotionally to images being cast onto a screen. That's literally all it was; an intense emotional reaction to light, images, and sound. None of what you witnessed was real. In fact, it was an entirely fictitious work that had been thought up in the creative mind of the screenwriter. Yet to your mind, everything that you witnessed felt real.

I recall two movies that affected me so deeply I couldn't leave the theater before composing myself. One was "Les Misérables," and the other was "Awakenings," based on the book by Oliver Sacks. In "Awakenings," Robert Deniro's character was afflicted by a condition called encephalitis lethargica. He had been in a deep sleeplike stupor, unable to respond to anything and anyone around him for 30 years. As a result of an experimental treatment, he suddenly awakens. Upon waking, he is so full of celebration and passion for life. It was a wonderfully feel-good part of the story and beautiful to watch. Sadly, the experimental drug's efficacy was only temporary, and he began to experience the condition's symptoms again. Only this time, he was aware that it was happening. He knew he was headed back into being trapped in his mind and body, unable to engage with any of his loved ones, possibly for the rest of his life. Everything was being taken away from him again.

I had a difficult time with that. It broke my heart, and at that moment, I became so unsettled and upset that I was sobbing in the theater. It was the type of sobbing you simply can't hide and draws attention. Not only was I reacting to the movie on the screen, but I was also reacting to the movie that was playing in my head about my father. You see, my father passed away when I was a freshman in high school. He had been diagnosed with leukemia when I was in 4th grade. He was a tall, strong man of Norwegian descent. He was insatiably curious and loved entrepreneurship. While he was going through treatments, he talked to me about the importance of visualization and meditation as a part of the treatment for his condition. And it paid off. He was fortunate to have been able to experience a remission of his condition. But it was temporary.

That is why I think the movie hit me so hard; my dad sinking back into illness was what I had just seen on the screen. My father had felt that same celebration while in remission. He was engaged in life and relationships at a high level for a short time. But then the symptoms of his illness returned. And for the very first time sitting in that theater, I gleaned some insight into what it may have been like for my father. He had beaten cancer and gained a new lease on life, only to see the cancer return aggressively. He always put on a brave face, even knowing he would return to the hospital for several weeks away from his family. He was optimistic and rarely let on that he was bothered by it. But I imagine his heart must have been breaking, knowing he wouldn't see his children grow up, he wouldn't meet his grandkids, or grow old with his wife. I imagine it must have felt soul-crushing at times.

The interesting thing is that neither the movie on the screen nor the scenario in my head was actually happening in the moment, in real-life. Even though it had been ten years since my father passed away, I developed a deeper understanding of him and his situation while watching the movie. It was a profoundly empathetic experience. I thought about it from his perspective as opposed to that of a 14-year-old. As a result, my brain had no choice but to create an intense emotional experience to match the intensity of the empathetic story unfolding about my father.

Our emotions determine the quality of every second of our lives. It blows me away when I think about it. Every emotion has a message, and I encourage you to pay attention and practice asking yourself, "What is the message of this emotion that I'm feeling?" The more you ask that question, the more you learn about yourself and those around you, even those that have passed on.

Stories, whether real or not, have a powerful effect on the brain. The brain creates a chemical reaction that **must** align with the story or meaning that we are focused on. It's really quite brilliant. What you focus on, you feel. And what's more, we don't just do this in the theater or when we watch a program on our laptop or phone at home. This is happening all day long. Our minds are constantly making up stories about ourselves, other people, work, the news, our finances, our sex lives, etc. We make up stories, and the brain supplies the emotional experience. When we say we feel sad, angry, happy, grateful, anxious, upset, or excited, it's because a chemical reaction that originated in the brain just coursed through our body in a millisecond. We feel the rush of adrenaline or dopamine or cortisol. And sometimes, the reaction is so intense that our body can begin to shake, sweat, produce tears, or change the way it is breathing. This can happen to the extent that we can feel lightheaded or have an incredible surge of energy.

THE KEYS TO THE KINGDOM

For me, understanding that "what you focus on, you feel" is like getting the keys to the kingdom. It means your emotional state is minimally affected by your physical situations and much more about where you place your focus. That's exciting. It means you can have an incredible amount of agency in how you feel. *You can determine how you feel!* Yes, it will take practice, but that's why it's called The Practice of Feeling Good. It's all about the practice.

Some people reading this may think, "Well, this sounds kind of impractical. Are you suggesting I ignore what is actually happening in the world and put my head in the sand?" I'm not suggesting that at all. In fact, I probably had my head in the sand for a good portion of my life, not noticing all the wonderful things happening in the world while I focused on the things that didn't feel good. I focused on what was not working out for me or the world. I focused on all the terrible things the news was reporting every day and all day. I would start my day with the news because I thought I was being responsible and staying informed. In reality, I was setting the emotional tone for my day! Then I would promptly share the disappointing and upsetting news with those around me, contributing to others feeling upset because I was getting them to focus on stories that didn't feel good. I focused on my shortcomings and the shortcomings of others. I focused on lack, injustice, and not getting my fair share. And how did I feel? I felt upset, insecure, fearful, anxious, and worried. My brain had no choice. It had to create a chemical/emotional response that matched the story I was focused on. I didn't want to feel this way.

But I felt this way regularly because I was practiced at placing my focus on stories that did not serve me and did not feel good.

We overwhelmingly focus on what's not working well, where we fall short, where our spouses or children fall short, on deficiencies in government, school, work, you name it. We're practiced at noticing inequities and things that don't go smoothly. We're practiced at focusing on the misses, the strikes, and the failures. We are highly practiced at creating disempowering stories, so we go through life feeling disempowered. People frequently share with me that they are dealing with feelings of discouragement, disappointment, disconnection, anxiety, stress, worry, fear, jealousy, insecurity, resignation, and hopelessness. It's time to do something radical.

Radical means a departure from what is normal, ordinary, or familiar. So a radical departure from focusing on disempowering stories would be to begin focusing on stories that do feel good and are empowering. Look for anything feel-good, no matter how small it is. In fact, practice going really broad, really general. Sometimes that is the easiest place to start. Did the sun come up today? Yes. That feels good. Is your heart pumping? Are your lungs breathing for you? Do you have mobility? Are you employed? Do you have friends or family around who care about you? Do you have a pet that brings you happiness? Look for anything that is working out in life. Focus on what is working well because what you focus on, you feel.

When we deliberately focus on an empowering story, the brain must respond by creating an emotional experience that aligns with the story. In doing so, you are beginning to shift your mindset. How would it feel to move from a mindset of financial scarcity to financial stability or even abundance? Or how would it feel to move from feeling stuck in your relationships to knowing that you have what it takes to transform them? How would it feel to move from self-doubt about starting the business you've always dreamed of to feeling absolutely certain you can do it? Imagine what would be possible in your health and fitness if your thoughts and emotions aligned with what you desired in life instead of focusing on where you are missing the mark. Would you have more energy or less? Would you have more motivation and inspiration?

If this sparks your interest, I invite you to read on because what lies ahead is the pathway for radically upgrading your mind. And I'm not talking about positive thinking. I'm talking about reorganizing your brain's circuitry, allowing you to take new actions and produce new outcomes that you didn't previously have access to in your life. It's exciting, feel-good work. I'll share my journey and some inspiring examples from my clients who have gone through this transforming work. The good news is that this can work for anyone, including you.

Key Takeaways

- What you focus on, you feel whether it is real or not.

- The brain creates a chemical reaction aligning with the story or meaning we are focused on, resulting in an emotional experience.

- Radical is a departure from what is normal, ordinary, or familiar. Our opportunity is to become radical by deliberately practicing bringing an empowering story to the present moment.

Opportunity to Practice

1. Identify and write down the most common emotions you experience during the day or week.

2. Do these emotions feel good? Do they move you forward or hold you back? Do they empower or disempower?

3. How would you like to feel on a more regular basis? Write down at least four emotions you would like to experience more often.

4. What stories, real or not, would you have to focus on to feel more of your desired emotions? Remember, the brain can't distinguish between what is real and what is not. You have artistic freedom here to create a story that feels good to focus on. Have fun with it! Pick at least two new stories and write them down. One of my favorites is that life always works out for my greatest evolution. This doesn't mean that I always get what I want or that life is working out how I expect it to. But it's working out for my greatest evolution. That means that even when it doesn't look, sound, or feel like life is working out at the moment, I can have certainty that whatever is occurring is contributing to my evolution in some way. There is something for me to learn, an opportunity to let go, contribute, grow or transform. It's a feel-good story.

5. What are a few feel-good stories that you enjoy focusing on and sharing with others? These might be fun stories that

families like to reminisce about when they get together. Or, they may be times in your life when you overcame an obstacle, hit a goal, or grew emotionally or spiritually. Think about those stories. How do you feel when you think or talk about them? Notice that you can feel certain emotions simply by focusing on the story.

6. Make a list of at least ten things that feel good in your life so you know what you can focus on more of the time. Examples: Feel-good music, inspiring shows or books, taking a walk, sitting in the sun, meditating, being early to the meeting, being prepared, cooking a favorite meal, connecting with friends, watching the sunrise or sunset, frolicking in the snow, watching your kids play, spending time with your lover. How many things can you come up with for your list?

3
SUFFERING VS. FEELING GOOD

"We all desire progress in our health, wealth, relationships, and general well-being. The Practice of Feeling Good is access to that progress."
- Fletcher Ellingson

Lisa is a veterinarian in a small rural town in Idaho. When we began working together, she had been running her business for over 30 years and was still in high demand. She was working six long days a week and taking emergency calls on top of that. Lisa has a big heart and is passionate about helping her animal clients. When I first sat down with her, it became clear that she was at a breaking point. She felt anxious, overwhelmed and had a considerable amount of self-doubt. Lisa didn't doubt her abilities as a vet but rather her ability as a business owner and creating a fulfilling personal life. In her own words, she felt like she was barely treading water and was in danger of going under. She felt alone in her business and didn't have much support in her career or personal life. While her business generated significant revenue, her accounts didn't show it, as there were many issues with the books, taxes, etc. After all, she was a veterinarian, not an accountant. She thought she had hired competent professionals. But it hadn't turned out to be the case. Lisa opened up her business to make a difference for animals and be in control of her time. She was undoubtedly making a significant difference for her clients but had zero freedom in the area of time.

It had also been a long time since she had a romantic partner, and she was skeptical that anyone was out there for her, especially in her small town. In fact, she was totally resigned and cynical about the possibility of ever finding a man with whom she could be happy. She didn't see any way out of the chaos of her life, the financial chaos, the business chaos, and the emptiness of her life outside of work. But one thing she was sure of, she couldn't go on like this anymore.

Lisa and I worked together for about a year. During that time, she came to understand several of the topics we are discussing in this book. As a result, she massively shifted her psychology and created new pathways in her brain that allowed her to think new thoughts, take new actions, and ultimately produce new results. I met up with her again recently, and she happily shared with me the changes in her life since going through the coaching curriculum of The Practice of Feeling Good.

First, she got her business finances in order, which was a huge relief. For years she believed she didn't have time to manage this area of her business. But she changed her belief around this to "There is always time for the things that are important to me." As a result, she was able to carve out time to research and hire a new bookkeeper to clean up the accounts and get the business back on solid footing.

She also created an empowering new belief around her love life. She used to believe no one was out there for her; a relationship was too much work, and she would be disappointed and likely get hurt. But her new belief was that a loving relationship was possible and on its way to her. And because she became open to the possibility of having love in her life again, she was able to create it. She met someone who treasures her and shares many of the same interests.

She created a new belief that her personal well-being was important and that it was imperative to prioritize herself instead of putting everyone else's needs in front of her own. She decided to take weekends off, which was a big deal and a huge relief after so many decades of nonstop work. Her new partner owns a plane and a motorcycle, so they get away for weekend adventures. She also decided to move from her longtime ranch, which required hours of mowing and all the other upkeep that goes along with owning a farm and animals. To Lisa's surprise, she easily qualified for a beautiful home in a nearby town with a pool. She sold her old ranch to her son, who had grown up on the property and was thrilled to take it over. It made her feel good to leave a legacy and keep that property in the family.

In short, as a result of intentionally upgrading her thinking, Lisa radically changed her life. Today, she's feeling optimistic, connected, valued, and hopeful. At our most recent visit, she hired me to help her further reduce her time in the clinic and consider her eventual exit strategy.

Lisa's story is familiar among entrepreneurs. They start a business because they are passionate about an idea, want to make a difference for their family and community, and are attracted to being their own boss. They want to call the shots and have freedom of time. But what frequently happens is that they are unprepared for everything required to run a business. They quickly discover it requires skills they don't have. They are required to wear many different hats they have never worn. They are suddenly the CEO, COO, CFO, HR, IT, head of marketing and sales, and maintenance. Talk about a demanding and intimidating job description! It's no wonder the vast majority of new businesses don't make it more than a few years. Opening up a business is not for the faint of heart.

So, let's dive into one of the most powerful distinctions, which was helpful for Lisa and has also been for all of my clients. This distinction has been around for a long time and has been discussed in several schools of thought. I'm sharing my own personal take on it. I was first introduced to this concept while going through one of the coaching curriculums of Tony Robbins. Then during my time in Legendary with David Bayer, we went even deeper into this work. It has been a game changer for me, and I believe it will be for you too. First of all, I suggest that there are two states of mind. And, given how our brains work, you can only be in one of those two states of mind at any given moment. For starters, let's look at one of those states, which we will call the "suffering" state.

THE "SUFFERING" STATE OF MIND

Although there are just two states of mind, there are many ways of being. Those ways of being will categorize you into one of the two states of mind. For example, if your way of being is angry, you will find yourself in a suffering state of mind. Other ways of being that result in a suffering state of mind include fearful, insecure, guilty, anxious, and jealous, to name just a few. We are all familiar with the suffering state of mind, and it doesn't feel good.

In the graphic below, you'll see many ways of being put us into a state of suffering. Notice that the arrows from the ways of being go directly into "suffering." This is because when we are in a suffering state of mind, we have very little energy to share. It's all about us. We become an energy drain. I bet you know someone in your life who, upon seeing them, makes you want to turn around and run because every time you see them, they give you an earful of the latest drama and everything that isn't going well in their life. These conversations don't leave you feeling empowered or energized- just drained.

SUFFERING STATE OF MIND

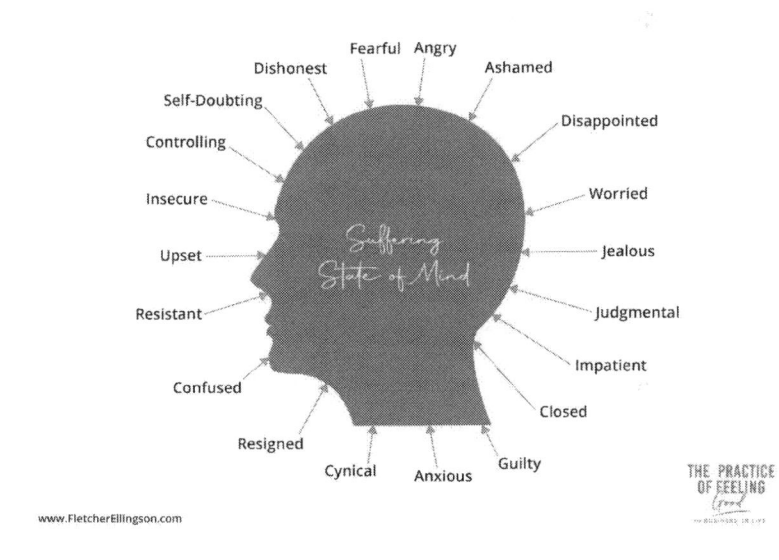

- Fearful
- Angry
- Dishonest
- Ashamed
- Self-Doubting
- Disappointed
- Controlling
- Worried
- Insecure
- Jealous
- Upset
- Judgmental
- Resistant
- Impatient
- Confused
- Closed
- Resigned
- Guilty
- Cynical
- Anxious

www.FletcherEllingson.com

As you look at this graphic, consider your day-to-day life. How many hours a day do you think you spend in the suffering state of mind? Be honest with yourself. One of the things you want to include is the time you spend driving. This is often a time when suffering is on display. You might realize that you fall into judgment and upset mode when someone cuts you off, or you feel they are driving too slowly. Some people feel anxious or worried while driving, while others use it as a time to dominate and act in ways they wouldn't typically if face to face with someone. We can experience a lot of suffering while behind the wheel of a car.

Look at all the ways of being that fall into a suffering state and ask yourself, "How many hours a day am I living here?" When I speak to an audience and ask them to shout out their numbers, I commonly hear eight to ten hours a day. Even if we lowball those numbers to six hours a day, multiply that by seven days, and we have 42 hours a week of suffering. Yikes, that's a full-time job…of suffering! That equals 168 hours a month operating in a suffering state. Not only is that time spent not feeling good, but you are also using up precious energy that could be spent on things you enjoy.

This is detrimental to the quality of our lives, especially when we think about what kinds of questions and self-talk we have access to when we are in a suffering state. When I'm suffering, my questions are rarely helpful or intelligent. They don't move me forward. My questions might sound like, "Why am I such a dumbass? Why can't I get it right? Why can't they get it right? Why is this happening to me?" And when I ask these types of questions, the brain has no choice but to answer.

The brain is like a search engine. It doesn't care what the question is. The only job it has is to go into the archives of your mind to find answers to the question you just asked- *exactly how you asked it*. If you ask, "Why am I such a dumbass?" your brain will undoubtedly find examples to support your inadequacies, compounding the suffering. It will bring up scenarios that make you cringe. Remember when you were in grade school and humiliated yourself in front of the entire class? How about that time you started a business, and it totally failed? Remember when you asked that girl out, and she said "No"? The brain doesn't judge your questions; its only job is to answer the question by supplying compelling evidence from the past. So the questions we have access to while we're in a suffering state usually hold us back. And then, if you look at the actions we have access to, you'll see those actions will likely align with the suffering state. And therefore, the actions will hold you back. "I can't figure this out; it will never work. I guess I'll just sit on the couch and binge Netflix instead of working on my business because I don't have what it takes."

Here is an important question I invite you to consider. What is the **cost** of your suffering? I encourage you to take a moment and really think about this question. In fact, as you consider it, get a journal and write down your findings. Really get curious about it and write it down so you can see it plainly in front of you.

What is the cost of your suffering? What does it or what has it cost you in your relationships? How about in the area of finances? What does it cost you in terms of your health and vitality? What does it cost you in your marriage? What does it cost you in terms of feeling empowered and worthy? What is the real cost of your suffering? I said earlier in this book that we're all very intelligent people. If that's true, and I believe it is, why are we suffering so much? Because wouldn't you agree that this suffering is getting in the way of us experiencing feel-good lives? Absolutely. Then why do we spend so much time suffering?

I'll share with you what I believe to be the answer. And when my clients understand this, they get a new lease on life. I hope this is the case for you. The reason we're suffering so much is that life is not matching up with the vision in our heads. We have a picture of how life *should* be. We have a picture of how our marriage, careers, bodies, parents, and children should be. Heck, we have stories about how the weather should be. We've envisioned these stories so many times and in great detail. When the physical reality doesn't match up, we feel disappointed, upset, jealous, impatient, frustrated, and often shut down. It doesn't feel good. We are in a state of suffering.

But here's what I want you to know. This is something I really want you to hear. **Almost all suffering is future or past based.** It is usually not about what is occurring in the moment. What do I mean by that? When you are worried or anxious, it is because you are thinking about what might happen in the future. And your brain doesn't distinguish between the now and the future very well. It doesn't differentiate well between what's real and what's not. And so it creates a chemical reaction called an emotion, and you feel it immediately. When you are focused on something in the future, you feel the emotion of that future-based scenario in the "now" moment. What you focus on, you feel, and what you focus on expands. What you focus on becomes your point of attraction, so you get even more of it. You may find yourself fearful or worried about something in the future that hasn't happened yet. But to the brain, it feels like it's already happening, which is why you get the emotional response in the now. So you will suffer anytime you spend time focusing on a future-based disempowering story.

The same goes for the past. Anytime you focus on and relive failures and traumas of the past, your brain will cue the correlating emotions, and you go into emotional suffering. Notice, all we are doing is thinking thoughts. This is how powerful our thoughts are! And this is what we do every day, on repeat.

It should go without saying, but the future and the past don't exist. Right? The past already happened, so we cannot go back and redo it. And the future has not happened yet. But the brain doesn't know that. So when you are reflecting on disappointing and upsetting stories, all the brain knows is that you're focused on it, and it must create an emotional response to align with the story you are viewing in your mind.

Let's say you fear speaking in front of an audience, but you have an upcoming event in two weeks that requires you to do so. As you envision that event, you begin to feel stressed as your brain increases your cortisol and adrenaline levels. You start to feel stressed and anxious in the moment, even though the presentation is two weeks away. You are experiencing a real emotional and, therefore, a physiological response to something you are simply imagining but is not actually happening.

I hope you'll read that a couple of times. Understanding how our brain works allows us to manage our emotional states better. We can begin to reduce our suffering by paying attention to and choosing where to place our focus. And that leads us to the next state of mind.

THE FEEL-GOOD STATE OF MIND

Recall that I said there are two states of mind. The second one is what I call the feel-good state of mind. There are various ways of being that allow you to enter this state. Take a look at the graphic below. I love this graphic. It's a reminder of where I want to spend more and more of my time.

FEEL GOOD STATE OF MIND

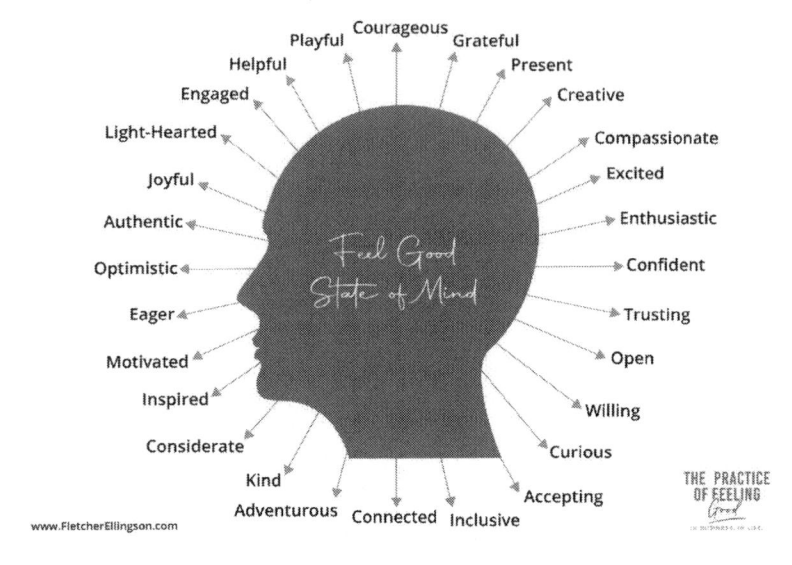

- Courageous
- Playful
- Grateful
- Helpful
- Present
- Engaged
- Creative
- Light-Hearted
- Compassionate
- Joyful
- Excited
- Authentic
- Enthusiastic
- Optimistic
- Confident
- Eager
- Trusting
- Motivated
- Open
- Inspired
- Willing
- Considerate
- Curious
- Kind
- Accepting
- Adventurous
- Connected
- Inclusive

www.FletcherEllingson.com

THE PRACTICE OF FEELING Good

You'll notice that in this graphic, the arrows are reversed. When you're operating from a feel-good state of mind, you aren't an energy drain; you have the energy to spare and share. You become a source of compassion, kindness, and contribution to other people. This is an incredibly empowering place from which to live life.

When operating from this place, what questions do you have access to? You have access to questions that move you forward. For example, "I'm not sure what the answer to this challenge is, but I know others have gone through it. Who can I reach out to for help or advice? Who can I model to get the results I want?" Your question goes from "Why is this happening to me?" to "How can I get through this, turn it around, and learn something from it?" And you will not only have access to powerful questions but powerful actions. You'll feel inspired, and inspiration always draws people into action. You will see advancement in your career and your relationships because the critical thing you have access to while operating from a feel-good state of mind is *progress*.

One of my clients, Paul, wanted to go on vacation with his family at least once a year. He wanted this badly but had not taken any vacations for several years. He felt really upset about it. When I asked him why he hadn't been taking them, he responded: "There's not enough time and money. And, there is no one to cover me at work. It's just not possible right now." He was in suffering. He worked hard to provide for his family and generate a great income, but he felt his hands were completely tied. Because he was operating from a suffering state, his mind automatically created thoughts that supported the idea that taking a vacation would be too expensive; there wasn't time for it, he couldn't find coverage, etc.

After talking for the better part of an hour, Paul slowly began to focus on how good a vacation would feel. He began to focus on what a gift it would be to his family. It would allow for connection, play, and rejuvenation, all of which he and his family needed. As we continued to focus on the feel-good parts of vacationing, he began moving out of suffering and into a feel-good state. And when he was fully in a feel-good state, we started asking forward-moving questions. For instance: "If you did have coverage, could you find the time to get away? If you had coverage and the time, could you find the money? If you could make it happen, would it be worth it? Would it provide wonderful memories? Would it be modeling the importance of family time to your children?"

We continued to ask forward-moving and feel-good questions until Paul could make a powerful new decision. He decided that he was resourceful, capable, and flexible. He decided that he didn't have to know the "how" right now to choose to go on vacation. He decided that it would work out. He decided it was important to him and that there was always time for the important things.

Two weeks later, I was checking in with Paul. We were talking about what was going well in his life. He was grinning from ear to ear when he told me he didn't just book one vacation but two week-long vacations and an additional four-day weekend getaway. His family was thrilled, and they were all getting resourceful in making it happen.

Operating from a feel-good state makes the difference. We all desire progress because it feels good. When you are operating from a place of suffering, there's a massive kink in the hose of progress. You can still make some progress, but it's usually diminished. But when you're operating from a feel-good state of mind, it feels like the kinks in the hose have been removed, and there is wide-open access to progress. You frequently feel like, "I'm in the zone!" You suddenly feel like things are coming together with greater ease. You can experience progress in your health, finances, relationships, or wherever you place your focus. And why do we want progress? Because it feels good!

So, how do you begin to live more from a feel-good state of mind? Well, it will take practice. But I will share with you where I start, where I ask my clients to start, and where I invite you to start. Expand your awareness of the concept of the two states of mind by noticing when you are suffering. Ask yourself, "Am I in a suffering or a feel-good state of mind right now?" Asking this question begins to interrupt the habitual program of suffering. It helps you become present in the moment. If you find that you're operating from a suffering state of mind, I recommend you go through the steps outlined in the *Opportunity to Practice* section below. It's the fastest way to move out of suffering and into a feel-good state of mind. And you will find the rest of the tools in this book are designed to help you operate more and more from a feel-good state of mind.

Key Takeaways

- There are two states of mind: A suffering state and a feel-good state.
- Our state of mind influences our questions, actions, and results.
- The reason we're suffering so much is that life is not matching up with the vision in our heads.
- A feel-good state of mind is access to progress.
- The fastest way out of suffering is to focus on gratitude.

Opportunity to Practice

1. **Practice gratitude.** Make a list of all the things going well in your life, the little and the big things. Notice everything that's going well. Are your lungs breathing for you? Yes, they are. You don't even have to tell them to do it. Is your blood circulating? Yes, it is. Do you have a roof over your head? Do you have food in the cupboards? You can be grateful for so many things: electricity, sunshine, paved roads, pets, transportation, smiles, connection,

love, technology, books, and so on. What else is there for which you can express gratitude? Really go for it!

2. **Visualize.** Visualize where you are heading and the progress you intend to make. Focus on that. What you focus on, you feel. The brain doesn't distinguish between what's real and what you imagine. But it will always create an emotional response that aligns with what you envision. So pick a good story, and get busy visualizing. Choose something inspiring that feels good because your brain will align with it and flood your body with all those feel-good chemicals. Once you have visualized it, your brain will store it as a memory of something that has already happened. In fact, when you go back to visualize it at a later time, you'll notice how much easier it is to visualize. Why? Because your brain has done it before. It remembers the visualization. It already stored it as a memory and then recalls the memory upon your request. It's brilliant! This is how you begin to live from a feel-good state of mind. It's all about taking baby steps. But these baby steps are critical. So get into action, have fun with it, and notice where life is working out for you.

3. **Breathe**. Today, we know more than ever about the importance of breath work. I am not an authority on this, so I am not spending time advising on breathwork practices in this book. But I do encourage you to check in with your breathing. When we are in suffering, our breathing is often shallow. Deep abdominal inhalations followed by slow and complete exhalations are incredibly effective for reducing the stress response. I encourage you to develop

some practice around this; even a small effort in this area makes a difference.

4. **Reminders.** Put a sticky note on your computer, bathroom mirror, or car dashboard that asks: "Am I suffering or feeling good?" Remember that increasing awareness of our mental state is key to influencing it. My wife used to set a few alarms on her phone to go off at different times of the day. When the alarm would go off, she would take a moment to get present and practice being grateful. If interested, there are a myriad of apps that you can use for this type of practice.

5. **Move.** That's right. Moving your body- whether walking, running, lifting weights, riding your bike, swimming, mowing the lawn, or even dancing in the living room- can help you move from suffering to feeling good. Moving our bodies promotes deeper breathing, better blood circulation, releases endorphins, and ultimately helps move us to a feel-good state of mind.

4

THE GIFT IN FEAR

*"Fear travels with an unseen gift, and
that gift is fear's kryptonite."*
- Fletcher Ellingson

Fear holds us back more than any other obstacle in life. And yet, I don't think fear is bad. It has a consistent and important message, "You may be in danger, pay attention." But fear is hyper-vigilant, tends to get very loud, and wants to run our thinking. The program has not evolved much over time and sees potential danger everywhere and in everyone. As a result, we get stopped in our progress and experience a lot of suffering. The more we understand fear, the more we will understand ourselves and why we make many of our decisions.

I invite you to consider the question: "What is at the center of fear?" When we understand what is at the center of fear, we can begin to navigate it much more powerfully. Notice I didn't say we could become fearless. I don't believe we can. I've never met anyone who is fearless. However, I believe we can experience less of it and move through it more quickly. To do so, we will need to become practiced at identifying the major types of fear and tapping into what I call "the gift in fear."

People have fear around a lot of different things. Some have a fear of flying or high places. Others have a fear of a relationship not working out. Many salespeople I know are dealing with a fear of rejection. And many people experience a fear of dying. While we have many fears, as far as I can tell, they all boil down to three types. Let's take a look at them. It's helpful to understand what they are so you can deal with them more quickly and effectively.

FEAR #1: FEAR OF NOT BEING GOOD ENOUGH

I believe the fear of not being good enough is the primary fear, the mother of them all. In fact, the other two are just different flavors of this one. But they occur uniquely enough in our thoughts that they are worth separating and distinguishing.

"Not being good enough" permeates our lives. It shows up in our friendships, sex lives, work, finances, hobbies, dreams, and aspirations. It shows up in our roles as parents and as children. The fear of not being good enough usually sounds a specific way. Here are a few ways you may have heard it in your own thinking: "I lack the knowledge or skills. I should be more like them and less like me. I'm too old or too young. I don't have what it takes. I can't because I'm fat, skinny, inexperienced, queer, slow, dumb, or (fill in the blank). I should be further along than I am. There's something wrong with me. I'm too emotional. I'm lacking something."

As you read on, remember the earlier question- "What is at the center of fear?" We'll answer that shortly, but I invite you to get curious. The fear of not being good enough runs deep in us. Even today, this fear still shows up regardless of all the work I've done on myself. However, my practice has allowed me to identify it much faster and move through it more effectively, and the intensity has been greatly diminished.

Around 2008 I became extremely well acquainted with this fear. Many of my friends were triathletes. They would frequently go out running, swimming, and biking. I was in awe at the levels of energy they had and what they were able to accomplish. Often they would invite me to go with them to participate in these activities. Each time I would laugh and scoff. I assured them I did not have what would be required to hang with them. I was sure of it in my mind. They were elite in their abilities. They had something special that I did not possess. They would tell me I was mistaken and that I did, in fact, have what it would take. Man, how I wanted that to be the case! They clearly didn't understand that I was mediocre at best.

Eventually, my wife, at the time, surprised me and started running and biking herself. I had never seen that side of her. She had never been an athlete. She didn't identify as an athlete. Yet there she was, consistently taking baby steps and increasing her distances. She began riding her bike to work while I drove. Then after entering multiple running events, she decided to sign up for a marathon. Wow, I was so inspired. I decided to give it a try as well. I started running and taking similar baby steps. I remember feeling proud that I ran 1.4 miles one evening; that was a big deal for me back then. Then I ran two miles and felt really accomplished when I hit three miles. Eventually, I hit five miles, knowing I was onto something.

My friends encouraged me to sign up for a multi-sport event.

It was an Olympic distance triathlon. It was a one-mile swim, a 26-mile bike ride, and a six-mile run. I knew I could do the run. But the bike and the swim? I could barely swim the distance down and back of a lap pool. But as I sat there and considered crossing the finish line, knowing how good I would feel, I agreed to sign up and immediately started training. Fast forward, I learned how to swim with the help of my friends. I bought a used bike and began going out with them on rides. I was always last, but I was going the distance. I became increasingly proficient in running, swimming, and biking. The day of the race came, and I had a blast. I was smiling practically the entire way. I discovered I actually had what it took to complete the event. Wow, that felt so good!

A few days later, my friend and I went on a bike ride. He told me he planned to sign up for the half Ironman distance the following year and asked me to do it with him. This distance was much greater than the one we completed several days ago. Interestingly, all the fears of not being good enough flooded back. I heard my thoughts as they came out of my mouth. "Oh, I couldn't do that. Those distances are way too far and require too much training." There I was again, defending my fear-based limitations. Fortunately, my friend just laughed and said, "Oh, you'll do it."

And he was right. The following year, we did it. I felt elated, strong, and powerful. And then, a few days later, on another bike ride, that same friend suggested we sign up for the full Ironman Triathlon the following year. What was my response? Fear again. You see, fear is always trying to keep us safe. It reminds us that we might be in danger and categorizes most things and people as dangerous. Wayne Dyer popularized the acronym for fear as "False Evidence Appearing Real." That always comes to mind when I begin feeling fearful. It's been so helpful in my life.

Long story short, I hemmed and hawed for a few weeks, defended my limitations, finally tapped into the gift in fear, and signed up for the Ironman Triathlon. It would be a 2.4-mile swim, a 112-mile bike ride, and a 26.2-mile run. I'll never forget that beautiful sunny day in Coeur d'Alene, Idaho. While my body was working hard, I was actually enjoying myself. It was challenging, but I felt inspired, and crossing the finish line was a game-changer. I had greater insight into what I was capable of accomplishing. What made the difference? The gift in fear. We'll get to it. It's coming.

FEAR #2: THE FEAR OF LOSS

Danny was in a state of massive suffering. As a real estate professional during the early months of COVID, he faced an entire set of unique challenges. He feared losing his career, savings, and life as he had known it. It weighed on him all day, every day. He watched the news constantly, waiting for hope, only to see things worsening. The infections, hospitalizations, and death rates were all climbing, and more restrictions were the norm.

He shared with me that he felt deeply fearful. I asked Danny if he had any leads that he could work on. I asked him if he had any clients or potential clients he could contact and check in with. He hesitated to reach out because he didn't want to appear insensitive and knew clients wouldn't want to meet during this time. I asked him how he knew that. He replied, "It's all over the news. Sales have come to a halt." I asked him if he had heard of any local sales in his industry. "Yes, there have been some, but not many," he replied. I asked him if he personally knew of any brokers who had completed transactions during this time to which he answered yes. So I said, "Do I understand that sales are happening and some people are willing to buy and sell during COVID?" He responded, "Yes, Fletcher. I know where you're going with this. But you don't understand. I don't want to offend my clients or blow the possibility of getting a listing by coming across as insensitive. Everyone is freaked out." I responded, "I hear that, Danny, and I respect that you want to be sensitive to your clients and potential clients. Would you be willing to go through an exercise with me?" He answered reluctantly with a big sigh, "Okay."

Over the next 45 minutes, we dove into what I call "the gift in fear." By the end of the exercise, Danny had reconnected to his primary mission: to help people navigate the complicated process of buying and selling a home to build greater wealth for themselves. He wanted to be of service to others. During our conversation, he also identified a person he wanted to contact about listing their home but had been too afraid to make the call.

As a result of our talk, Danny committed to calling that person right after we got off the phone. About 60 minutes later, I got a call from Danny. He was thrilled. He made contact with the homeowner and learned that they had wanted to list their waterfront home. But then COVID hit, and they were unsure how to proceed, therefore, hadn't taken any action. Danny was in a perfect position now to guide them through the new processes. He got the meeting, the listing, and the home sold within a couple of months. Danny had a fantastic new client, and selling the $1.2 million home netted him $35,000. It was definitely worth his while to learn how to manage his fear.

There are real costs to being ruled by our fears and real payoffs when we tap into the gift in fear. (Hold on, we're getting there).

Danny's fear of losing clients by offending them or coming across as insensitive was taking him out of action. His fear of loss ironically ensured that he would lose by keeping him out of the game. We frequently take actions or inactions based on the fear of loss. We might not take a risk for fear of losing money. We might not ask a question or say no to a person's request for fear of losing respect. We may put off having that honest conversation for fear of losing a friend. We may stay too long in a particular job or relationship for fear of losing security. The fear of loss is powerful and can have incredibly steep costs.

Remember, I said that the fear of not being good enough is the mother of all fears. The fear of loss is linked to not being good enough. If I lose my fortune, partner, health, or respect, that somehow makes me not good enough. And if I'm not good enough, people may not accept me. And if I'm not accepted, then it feels like dying. It sounds dramatic. But that is how it can feel.

FEAR #3: THE FEAR OF FAILURE

The summer between my first and second year of college, I took a position in a sales call center. We were selling subscriptions for season tickets to a local theater. I thought the job would be easy. You just had to read a script and improvise a bit. How hard could it be?

Well, I soon found out the hard part was dealing with rejection. I was taking it all personally, and it felt terrible. I was utterly fearful that I was going to fail with each call. Every time I picked up the phone, I was terrified of being told no, and I lasted all of three days at that job. To top it off, I feared looking like a fool in front of my boss. So one day, I called and lied to him instead of going to work. I told him I had contracted Mono and didn't know how long I would be sick. So it would be best for him to plan on me not returning. I can laugh at it now as I recall the event. But at the time, I felt so ashamed of my behavior.

Many of my clients are entrepreneurs, and one of their biggest fears is failing. It's understandable. Some stats indicate that nearly 50% of small businesses fail within one year of launching, and 95% fail within five years. My hat is off to those who take action because, for every person who does take bold action on their dreams, many others do not. The fear of failure can be so intimidating that we decide to play it safe and risk never finding out how powerful and wonderful we are. As with the fear of loss, this fear of failure is just another flavor of the fear of not being good enough. We fear that if we do fail, we won't have what it takes to reinvent ourselves. We fear we are somehow lacking; we're not good enough. And because we've listened so many times to these thoughts, it feels like the truth.

The good news is that it's not the truth. You are good enough, always have been, and always will be. All that you need is within you. It's a matter of trusting this and leaning into it. And it takes practice.

WHAT IS AT THE CENTER OF FEAR?

Anytime you feel fear, you can begin to interrupt it by asking yourself: "Am I fearful of losing something or someone? Do I fear failure? Or am I fearful I'm not good enough for the person or situation before me?" When we get curious about our fears, we *interrupt* the fear program. Getting curious about our fear creates space between us and the fear. In that space, we can begin to navigate with more presence of mind. Now, let's turn our attention to the question I asked earlier: **What is at the center of fear?** Once we understand this, we can deal more powerfully with our fear. We can diminish it, reduce the volume, and begin to take action despite it.

So here it is. At the center of fear, there is simply a *story*. That's it. A story. This story feels like the truth. But it isn't the truth. It's just a story we created at some point in the past, often unknowingly and while in fear. And we are intensely focused on it. It's a "worst-case scenario" about what might happen. You see, fear is always future-based. The story that fear presents us is a narrative about what might happen in the future. The future doesn't exist. This means we are having an emotional and physiological response to something that isn't actually happening. What you focus on, you feel. Your brain must create an emotional experience that aligns with what you are focusing on. When you focus on a fear-based story, you will experience fear, your heart rate will increase, you can begin to sweat, shake, and your mouth can go dry, all because of the story you are focusing on. At the core of fear is a story.

This is terrific news. Why? Because we can deal with a story. How? By changing it. We have the ability to change the story. And this brings us to the gift in fear.

THE GIFT IN FEAR

Fear always travels with a gift. That gift, should we accept it, is the opportunity to be courageous. Several years ago, I was faced with a chance to be courageous when it came to financially investing in myself. I've always read personal development books, listened to audios, and attended seminars. Those are all wonderful ways of investing in myself. But, at this particular time in my life, I needed more help to really move the needle. I needed to be immersed in the conversation, have a higher level of accountability, and have people who believed in me and challenged me. That would require a big investment and more than I had been willing to spend up until then. The most I had ever spent on a program was $10,000, which was a big stretch. The program I really wanted to be a part of was $25,000 for one year.

My wife and I had flown to Florida for a three-day seminar called The Powerful Living Experience, which David Bayer and his fantastic team put on. When the offer to invest in the premium program was presented at the end of the weekend, I crossed my arms and was resolute that I would not do it. No way. But the thing was, I really wanted to do it. There was a quiet voice in my head rooting for my greatness and urging me on, even though I didn't want to listen to it. I was coming up against my fear, big time. I was fearful of being duped. I was fearful that it was an irresponsible use of my money. I didn't think I was worth it. And, when I listened closely, my biggest fear was that I would spend all of this money and nothing would change, that it wouldn't make a difference for me. Yep, I was in massive suffering.

I felt so stuck. I wanted to do this, but my fear had me arguing for my limitations. At that point, I wanted to leave the conference. I could barely stay in my seat; I just wanted to escape this conflict in my head. Fortunately, two very influential people helped me step into courage and consider the quieter voice. The first was my wife, who emphatically encouraged me to sign up. She had no fear about it and trusted that it would be what I needed to help me get to that next level in my life professionally and personally. She reminded me of all the reasons I should do it. She painted a feel-good story that was radically different from my fear-based story and told me she was 100% supportive.

The other person at the conference who influenced me was Sean Stephenson, a well-known therapist, author, and speaker. I'll never forget what Sean said while up on stage. It felt like he was talking directly to me. He said, "Stop being so stingy. You have something to share with the world. Trust the universe and share it." So with the support and prompting of my wife and Sean's words in my head, I decided to invest in myself at a new level. I decided that what I was committing to was not just for me, but it was for my family. I would be a better husband and better father. I would be a better friend. I would serve my existing and future clients at a higher level. I went from being stuck in my seat, gripped by fear to seeing this course as a way to achieve my personal and business outcomes. And that entire process happened in my head as I went from a suffering, fear-based story to a feel-good, courageous story. I spent four years in that program, and it was worth every dollar and will continue to pay dividends for life.

Let's look at another example. Firefighters who run into a burning building to rescue people are not necessarily doing so without fear. They have fearful stories in their heads. But they're not stopped by the stories because they intentionally create a different narrative than the fear-based story that their mind automatically generates. Instead, they create a story that says, "We are prepared to go into that house." They focus on the fact that they are well-trained for the situation. They remind themselves and each other that they have what it takes. The story they play out in their heads shows them getting into the house, rescuing the people, and getting out safely. It's a feel-good story. And that story triggers a different emotional experience and produces a different outcome. It allows the firefighters to take action and navigate dangerous situations.

Courage is the gift in fear, and it is fear's kryptonite. Just like kryptonite weakens Superman, courage weakens fear's grip on us. But how do we step into courage? First, we must ask the familiar question: "What is at the center of courage?" That's right—a story. At the center of courage, there is simply a different story. Where does it live? It, too, is future-based. But this story requires us to be present and intentional. The fear-based story is automatic, and the mind creates it without our permission. It excels at doing this; it's practiced at doing it. The courageous story is yours to create and will lead you down your chosen path.

At the core of The Practice of Feeling Good is the practice of bringing an empowering, feel-good story to any situation. Creating a feel-good story in the face of our fears allows the brain to focus on something other than our fear. Unless we generate a different story for the brain to focus on, it can only focus on the story of fear. You've heard the famous quote(s) attributed to Franklin D. Roosevelt, Nelson Mandela, Mark Twain, and many others. There are variations, but it goes something like this: "Courage is not the absence of fear, but rather the assessment that something else is more important than fear." Our ability to generate a courageous story is critical.

Key Takeaways

- There are three main types of fear: Fear of not being good enough, fear of failure, and fear of loss.
- The message of fear is you may be in danger and to pay attention.
- At the core of fear, there is a future-based story.
- At the core of courage, there is also a future-based story.
- The gift in fear is the opportunity to be courageous.
- Courage is fear's kryptonite.

Opportunity to Practice

1. Can you identify any fears holding you back or causing you suffering? What are they? Write them out in detail so you can begin to understand them better.
2. What has been the cost of having these fears? Have you missed out on opportunities or experiences? Has there been a financial or health cost?
3. Which category of fear do they fall into? Fear of not being good enough, fear of failure, or fear of loss? Remember, some fears may fall into two or even all three categories.
4. What is the story at the center of these fears? Notice that it is future-based. Also, notice that it feels like the truth.
5. Next is the opportunity for courage. Remember, the fear-based story is not accurate. You get to create a new feel-good story, a courageous story. Write it out. Use plenty of details so your brain can picture it clearly. Get your body

involved. Stand up and read it aloud to yourself with conviction every day so your brain stores it as a memory and begins to reference it easily. It may feel silly, but this is the beginning of creating a new program your brain can use. You can do this, and I believe in you.

5

THE PRACTICE OF OVERCOMING AN UPSET

There is a message in every single upset. Once you understand the message and the main causes of an upset, you can navigate them with a greater sense of ease. Moving through an upset powerfully is not commonly taught, nor something most of us saw growing up or currently see modeled for us. We are used to seeing upsets met with anger, accusation, defensiveness, withdrawal, judgment, resentment, or retribution.

Upsets are a part of life. There's no getting around this fact, and The Practice of Feeling Good will not eliminate upsets from our lives. However, from personal experience and my client's experiences, I can tell you that the frequency of upsets can be significantly diminished, the intensity reduced, and the duration shortened. Upsets don't feel good, but they will happen and do not mean anything is wrong with us. In fact, upsets carry important messages. If we learn to understand and pay attention to the messages, we can get back on track, progress, and feel better faster.

THE MESSAGE OF AN UPSET

What is the message of an upset? The ultimate message is that something is not how you want it to be. Being present to the message is the first step to exiting the suffering mindset and making your way back to a feel-good mindset. From years of studying with mentors, attending seminars, and personal inquiry, I've learned that every upset falls into one or more of just a few categories. When we understand this, we have access to a powerful opportunity. The opportunity is to change the story on which we are focused. This is important because that which we focus on, we feel. Remember the example of watching a movie in the theater? Your brain has no choice but to create a chemical reaction or emotion that aligns with the story you are focused on. So when I say, "What you focus on, you feel," I mean it quite literally.

Most of the stories we focus on are created in the time it takes you to snap your fingers. They are created without our permission, consent, or approval. The brain doesn't give us a menu of options; it chooses for us based on our programming, which has been with us since we were young. So the meanings we bring to any situation are largely habitual, frequently don't feel good, and often don't serve us. For the purposes of our conversation, we are going to focus on what I believe are the three main causes of an upset. Let's examine them to learn how to handle them more effectively.

CAUSE #1: THE FRUSTRATED OR UNMET EXPECTATION

If you look closely, you will see that we almost always have an expectation about how something should happen, even when we are not consciously aware of this expectation. And, when we have expectations of others, ourselves, or situations that are unmet, we experience an upset. "I expected them to be on time, but they were late. I expected a raise during my review but didn't get one. I expected the weather to be sunny for the outdoor event, but it poured rain. I expected my health, wealth, relationships, etc., to look differently than they do."

As defined by www.dictionary.cambridge.org, the verb "frustrate" means *to prevent the plans or efforts of someone or something from being achieved.*

Years ago, my client, Jose, was in a business relationship with some partners who chose not to honor his contract when it came time for him to depart the company he had helped build. This was surprising to him. He fully expected these people to act with integrity, so he felt upset and disappointed when that expectation was unmet. He had poured his heart and soul into building the business and cared about his clients, legacy, and future financials. The situation was quite a blow. His mind wasted no time and got to work creating story after story about how he was right and how they were wrong. It kept presenting images of how much money he was losing, how he was being taken advantage of, and how he was the victim. It presented scenarios of going to court and other ways of getting even. None of what his mind was showing him felt good. In fact, it felt terrible. Yet his mind continued to go over and over the same thoughts, not caring about the emotional toll it was causing him.

We both knew he was in a state of deep suffering. So we took out our mindset tools and got to work. At the core of The Practice of Feeling Good is the practice of replacing a disempowering story with an empowering and feel-good story. We constructed a new narrative. The new story said that while these people were not acting with integrity, they were doing their best with the tools they had and the programs running them. I don't mean this as "One person is better than another." I really do believe Jose's business partners were doing their best from their point of view. Jose would have behaved the same way if he were in their shoes and had their programming. Knowing they were doing their best allowed for judgment to subside and made way for understanding, empathy, and compassion.

Now, I also believe holding people accountable without a desire for punishment or retribution is possible. However, pursuing legal action and the drama accompanying it was not the outcome Jose desired. Therefore, we had to create a story that felt so good it would be easy for him to let go and move on. He decided that the future was full of opportunities that would be realized sooner if he let go of the blame, victimization, and drama. He concluded that this was one of those defining moments in a person's life that rarely comes around. The kind of moment that can break you or make you stronger. He wanted to be stronger. We agreed that this was an opportunity to trust at a deeper level and that he would become wiser, stronger, more compassionate, and more understanding as a result. In doing so, he would be required to leave his comfort zone. And we all know from experience that this is where the magic happens.

Jose could create with even more intention and enthusiasm by allowing himself to move on. He decided to put out even greater value in his next venture as a consultant. And as a result of that value, he would positively impact people, make a difference in the world, and be well compensated. He told me that if he could focus on creating and executing this new vision, life would be better than ever and genuinely feel good. And that's what happened. He let go of the old story, embraced the new one, and launched a career that inspired him and his clients. And to this day, Jose is living his best life.

That's the power of The Practice of Feeling Good in action. Many of our expectations will be frustrated or completely unmet. As a result, we will experience an upset. But I want you to know that the upset doesn't mean anything is wrong with you or anyone else. It simply means something isn't happening as we expected. We can choose to practice blame and victimization or decide to practice curiosity and be resourceful, capable, and flexible.

The COVID pandemic provided several years of dealing with frustrated expectations. People expected to be able to have weddings, funerals, sporting events, or vacations only to be told they had to cancel them. We all expected to do things, see people, and live life as usual. But mandates severely frustrated our expectations during those COVID years.

When you experience a frustrated or unmet expectation, it is because something gets in the way of achieving your desired outcome. During COVID, we frequently had to practice bringing an empowering story to many situations. My wife and I had spent months planning to host a personal development seminar. We rented event spaces, hired a catering company, and purchased all sorts of items for the attendees. We were excited to spend time with the people who had purchased tickets to join us for a weekend full of learning and connection. But just days before we were scheduled to meet, the world began shutting down…quickly.

I felt very disappointed. And I remained disappointed for several weeks. Like many people, I asked myself, "What does this mean for my business and my mission to help make a difference for people?" At first, it appeared very bleak. So I had to remind myself of my feel-good compound: "I am resourceful, capable, and flexible." If those were my primary ways of being, I could do anything. I began asking myself empowering questions. "What would it look like to do the seminar online via Zoom? Could I condense and spread the content out over eight two-hour sessions instead of three days? How could I get creative and still offer massive value to my clients?"

And as we all know now, this is what many businesses adopted and made it work. We asked empowering questions which led to empowering actions and results. While there was a lot of suffering during the COVID years, there were also incredible displays of ingenuity and creativity. If people can navigate through their upsets, the opportunity to create is on the other side waiting for them.

Many of us decided the COVID shutdown was an opportunity to spend more time with our immediate families. It was an opportunity to slow down. As a result of less in-person connection with the world, we realized how much we really did appreciate and need connection. Our children learned how much they actually appreciated in-person school. And while there was a lot of division in the world, there was also a beautiful amount of global unity. We focused on that story a lot in our household. COVID was an incredible time to practice creating empowering, feel-good stories in the face of many frustrated and unmet expectations.

Again, we can't eliminate upsets, but we can navigate them more effectively and become stronger and wiser in the process. It all comes down to our awareness of what is happening in our thinking and moving forward with a feel-good story.

CAUSE #2: THE MISCOMMUNICATION

We are in communication with people all day long. We make plans, pick dates, set times and interact while at work, at home, or at play. Sometimes the communication lands as we intend, and other times it misses. It may miss by an inch or a mile.

An easy example of this is to imagine you are having a dinner party. You have invited a couple of your friends for a fun evening of dinner and games. You let them know that dinner will be ready at 6:00 pm. As you finish a few tasks, you look at your watch. It's now 6:05. You think, "No worries, they will be here any second." You check your watch a few minutes later. It's 6:10, and still, no car in the driveway, no calls or texts. By 6:15, you begin to feel upset, "I clearly told them 6:00 pm. This is so rude. The least they could do is call." You decide to call them, but there is no answer. You feel disrespected.

At 6:23, your mind begins to spin a different scenario. "They are really late. I wonder if they're okay. I wonder if they got in an accident. The weather's pretty bad out there." You're upset, and now you take on worry along with feeling disrespected and frustrated about being unable to reach them.

Finally, at 6:26, the doorbell rings. You answer the door feeling upset and ready for an explanation. When you open the door, your friends are there with smiles and a bouquet of flowers. They come in, hug you, and act as if nothing is wrong. They offer no apology for running late. And still feeling upset and wanting some answer for their running late, you say, "Gosh, I was getting worried. Did you run into traffic or something?" They look confused, "What do you mean? I thought we were right on time?"

It becomes clear that they thought they were on time for the 6:30 dinner party. In fact, that time *had* been discussed, but you felt sure you all had agreed on 6:00. This is a common occurrence and an example of how miscommunication frequently leads to an upset. It doesn't have to, but remember, the mind is a master when creating stories without your permission. That's what it does. It continuously cranks out stories without your consent or approval. It comes up with a juicy story and says, "Print it!" without fact-checking or getting it approved. Then the brain creates the corresponding emotion. And it all happens in the blink of an eye.

Imagine that same situation again. If you had been present to the story, your emotion, and your suffering, you could have interrupted it. You may have thought, "Whoa, there goes my mind creating stories again. Whoa, there goes my body having an emotional reaction to my stories." At that point, you could begin to operate outside of the program. "I trust my friends are going to make it here. Maybe they hit traffic. Perhaps they don't have cell reception. Maybe they got the times mixed up. I can be flexible. This is all going to work out. We'll still have an enjoyable evening."

Wow, what a different story, right? And if that's the story you focus on, you will have a different emotional experience. In this version of the evening, you would have been able to meet them at the door with an open heart and have no barriers to having a great evening with people you love.

Again, this takes practice. But it's worth it.

CAUSE #3: FEAR-BASED SILENCE

As I mentioned, sometimes we become upset because a situation doesn't unfold as we wish. But quite frequently, we experience an upset because we don't speak up. We are gripped by a fear-based silence. We hold back an important communication because we feel insecure and fearful about voicing it. Maybe we're afraid we will be judged. Perhaps we worry we won't be articulate and will embarrass ourselves. We fear that we may be rejected or lose status. You can see that; ultimately, we can trace this back to the fear of loss and the fear of not being good enough.

Sometimes we even withhold something because we tell ourselves the other person can't handle it. Holding back our communication doesn't serve us because we're left feeling like we don't have a say in things. We give up our power, feel misunderstood, feel like a victim, and as a result, can feel resentful.

What story is at play here that would create this situation? The story may sound like this, "They don't value my opinion. They won't understand me. My ideas always get shot down. They can't handle the truth. They'll get upset or defensive." Those are just a few stories that keep us from delivering certain communications. What we're really doing is disempowering other people. We are making *them* small; we're saying *they* can't handle it or *they* won't understand. As a result, we clam up and suffer. And all because we are not practiced at expressing ourselves. And believe me; I get this loud and clear. I have wrestled with and still wrestle with this one. It requires a lot of practice!

We must change the story to move from suffering to a feel-good state of mind. Imagine if our stories sounded more like the following: "My opinion matters, and they must have an opportunity to hear it. Even if they don't agree or like what I have to say, I can remain open and trust we can work it out. I am confident they can handle what I have to say."

Remember, when we choose and focus on a story, our emotions will correspond. You can begin to feel confident, courageous, or enthusiastic. And doesn't that feel better than remaining locked in fear-based silence? Voicing your truth will take courage, along with practice. Remember, it's not about being or doing it perfectly. It's about creating meaningful connections, which always feels good.

THE FOUR C METHODOLOGY

Now that we understand the main causes of an upset, let's discuss what I call the Four C Methodology. This methodology is a step-by-step way to move through the upset once you have identified that you are upset and understand the cause of it.

The First C: Calm

When we are in an upset, our body releases greater levels of adrenaline and cortisol. The result can be shallow breathing, feeling shaky, foggy thinking, and a desire to run away, shut down, or attack. So, the most important thing to do first is to get calm to begin managing our thinking and actions. The quickest and simplest way to get calm is to regain influence over our breathing. If the situation allows, find a quiet place for some deep belly breaths. Take nice big inhales followed by long full exhales. Do this for a couple of minutes. This brings needed oxygen to your body and brain, diminishing the shakiness and foggy thinking. It also stimulates your parasympathetic nervous system, which counteracts your fight-or-flight response.

Another thing you can do is go for a short walk or move your body in some way. This creates a change in your physical state which interrupts your unconscious programming that is running. This first step is also going to prepare you to be able to move into the second C.

The Second C: Curiosity

Getting curious about the situation instead of judging it is an essential part of moving through an upset faster and easier. Getting curious means asking forward-moving questions about ourselves, others, and the situation. For instance, a common example for many of us would be getting upset at the driver in front of us for driving five or six miles beneath the speed limit. We may find ourselves swearing under our breath or even out loud. We may roll our eyes or throw our arms in the air as if to say, "What the heck? Hurry up already!" Or perhaps you have been on the receiving end of another person's unkind behavior as they pass you, which can then result in you feeling upset.

Getting curious in this situation would look like asking the following questions: "I wonder what is going on for that person?" As a result of asking the question, you are able to consider answers that are not based in judgment and allow you to feel calmer. You come up with several possible answers. Maybe they have a cup of hot coffee between their legs, so they are driving more conservatively. Perhaps they were recently in an accident and are being extra careful. Maybe their speedometer is not correctly calibrated. Perhaps they think the speed limit is something different than what is posted. Maybe they recently had surgery and are driving at a speed that produces less vibration and feels better. Or perhaps they simply are not paying attention to their speed at this moment. Whatever the actual answer is, we won't know. The point of the second C is to practice getting curious about what is going on for others and begin to interrupt the upset.

We also want to get curious about what is going on for us. We can ask, "Why am I frustrated and upset that this driver is going slower than I want them to go? Am I going to be late for something important? Am I making up a story that driving below the speed limit is inconsiderate and rude? Am I worried that the people behind me will think I am a slow driver and inconsiderate? Am I simply practiced at being impatient and judgmental of others? Do I really think that person is inconsiderate and rude, or is my brain reacting habitually? Who is in control here, me or my program? Can I relax and be ok with being behind a slower driver? Will this really impact my day and my life?" Getting curious is an important way of being when navigating any upset, whether it is with your co-worker, spouse, business partner, family member, the government, or a slow driver. And it prepares you for the third C.

The Third C: Courage

You will recall from the chapter on fear that a story is at the center of fear. This story usually tends to hold us back and keep us small. In fear, we shrink away from life rather than engage it. The story may be that I might upset someone if I am self-expressed. Or fear may say that you are at risk of being rejected, mocked, embarrassed, unpopular, etc. When you find yourself fearful about communicating, remember the gift in fear is the opportunity to be courageous.

At the center of courage, there is simply another story. But it is an empowering story. If you are fearful about speaking up or expressing yourself, create an empowering courageous story. It may sound like this: "What I have to say has value. What I have to say matters. What I have to say may be helpful for someone else as well. I can handle whatever response I receive. I am becoming more and more practiced at speaking up for myself. It feels good to contribute my ideas and ask my questions. I'm becoming better and better at articulating my thoughts. They can handle what I have to say. We can work through any difficult conversations."

If this is our story, it will be much easier to practice sharing our concerns, requests, questions, and suggestions. It will take practice, but think about how good it will feel to speak with confidence and certainty. And when you are operating from confidence and certainty, you move to the fourth C, where things get really exciting.

The Fourth C: Creating

I had been avoiding the conversation for years. I did not think I had it in me to say what needed to be said. I was afraid I would upset this person if I were honest about my feelings. I thought that I would upset the family dynamic if I were honest. And because I had given into the influence of fear for years and kept my thoughts and emotions to myself, I began to resent this particular person. That resentment consumed my energy whenever I had to be around or talk about him. Richard was a member of my extended family, and I had to spend time with him at all the family get-togethers. I had constructed so many disempowering and negative stories about him. I became highly practiced at judging him and avoiding him at all costs. But one August weekend, we were in the same room at a personal development seminar.

I didn't want to be there with him, but I was glad he was there. I thought maybe he would hear something and transform himself, making my life easier. Perhaps he would have a breakthrough, and then he would reach out to make amends. Maybe he would change so I could drop all my resentment and feel better. Yeah, if he changed, my life would be better.

Well, things didn't happen the way I expected. The breakthrough came for me. I realized that my upset was exactly that… mine. I realized that my resentment, judgment, and disdain were of my own making. I saw clearly that my communication patterns had me feeling trapped and suffering. I had never once actually brought any of my concerns to this man. I had never given him a chance because I had accused, judged, convicted, and sentenced him already in my mind. I had created a disempowering story about him; all I did was gather evidence to support my story. When I saw what I had done, I knew I had to take responsibility for it. My brain attempted to stop me. It started justifying all my past behaviors and pointed out that I had been right to keep it all to myself. After all, whatever I would have said wouldn't have made a difference. In fact, it would have made things worse. I was right to have remained silent and judgemental. Yep, it's not pretty, but this is what our brain does to keep us safe and right. But that weekend, I knew what I had to do.

During a meal break, I ran to the store for a quick bite to eat, but all I could think about was the conversation I knew I had to have with Richard. My stomach became so upset I couldn't even eat the meal I had just purchased. I began shaking and crying from fear and self-doubt. Can I do this? I had to step into courage and come up with a new empowering story. And that is what I did. I decided that Richard was doing his best with all of his programming, just like I was doing my best. I decided I didn't know what it was like to be in his shoes with his upbringing and the challenges he had faced and was still facing.

I gathered evidence supporting the story that he was doing his best. And it was actually easy to find. As a result, I began to feel compassion for him. I started seeing that so many of his actions and things that he had said were coming from a very wounded young boy who was physically all grown up but whose wounds had never healed. In a flash, I saw his entire complicated life centered around coping with tremendous adversity, insecurity, and a desire to feel loved and accepted. It all became clear, and I knew what I had to do. I had to create a new chapter in our relationship for me and my family.

I found him in the building getting ready to attend the next seminar and asked if I could talk with him for a few minutes. As soon as I began speaking, the tears started to flow. I apologized for judging him harshly and told him how it had poisoned me and our relationship. I told him I had been blaming him and making him wrong for all sorts of things in our family. And I told him that those thoughts and behaviors ended that day. I also acknowledged him for so much support and love I had seen him display for his family. I let him know that he could count on me to be honest with him. I told him I might disagree with him, likely frequently, but he could count on me to be honest and open and accept him rather than judge him. He didn't lash out or attempt to belittle me, to my surprise. Instead, he began to cry as well. He appreciated my honesty and courage and the acknowledgment that I shared with him. He welcomed the opportunity to create a fresh start.

It was a breakthrough for me and a breakthrough for us. Even though I had yet to identify the 4 Cs, I was using them. I had to get to a place of being somewhat calm. I had to get curious about how life had been for this man. I had to step into courage. And then, finally, create an empowering story and a new relationship with him. Was it always smooth sailing after that? No, but it was much better, more honest, and I could view him as someone doing his best just as I was doing my best. And that feels way better than judgment, anger, and disdain.

The fourth C, creating, is an exciting opportunity. It is where you arrive after working all the way through an upset. Once you have navigated the steps of being calm, curious, and courageous, you can create! You can ask yourself, "What do I want to create around this issue? What do I want to create with this person? What do I want to create with my family? What do I want to create with my community?" Have fun with this part; it is where you assert creative license with your life.

Key Takeaways

- The message of an upset is that something is not the way you want it to be.
- Three of the main causes of an upset are:
    - A frustrated or unmet expectation
    - A miscommunication
    - Fear-based silence

- Using the 4 C Methodology will help you navigate upsets faster and more effectively.

Opportunity to Practice

Where are you feeling upset in your life? Write down at least two real-life examples to use with the following questions.

1. Which of the three categories does the upset fall into? (It may fall into any or all of them).
2. Implement the 4 C Methodology. How does it allow you to see the situation differently? What is the new and empowering story you can bring to the situation?

Remember, the new story may not feel real. That's okay. Continue to focus on the new story, and the mind will eventually fall in line with it. It's all about the practice.

6

YOUR VALUES DON'T MEAN JACK

I don't think my values, your values, or our collective values mean jack. You might be thinking, "What is this guy talking about? Of course, values make a difference- we all have values, and they help guide us!" I understand that perspective because I used to feel the same way.

Companies hold meetings and retreats in the business world to "establish their core values to guide the company forward." And many people feel strongly about their personal values. I am not saying there is zero benefit in examining these values. But, there is a misconception that knowing company values will make a difference in sales, production, and company culture. There is a misconception that focusing on personal values will improve relationships, finances, health, and fitness. It will not. I am including this conversation in this book because many people believe that having feel-good values equates to a feel-good life. It does not. Stay with me, and I'll demonstrate what I mean. We'll also answer the next logical and exciting question: "If my values don't move the needle, then what does?"

Imagine walking down a crowded street, stopping and asking random people to list their values. You would see lists that contain many of the same words, such as family, honesty, strong work ethic, collaboration, creativity, contribution, financial security, health, fitness, mobility, education, integrity, trust, loyalty, and innovation. And the list goes on. If you look at various companies' values, which I have, you will see similar lists. So individuals and companies seem to value the same things. But even after companies determine their core values and share them with their teams, they are often left wondering why there is still a noticeable gap between those values and the actual results the teams produce.

When we look at single people searching for someone to share their lives with, they say, "I want to find someone who shares the same values as me." They assume that if they find this partner, the relationship will go more smoothly and produce favorable results. But I am suggesting that we all share the *same* values with very few exceptions, albeit in varied levels of importance. If I were to ask twenty strangers from different parts of the world if they value family, health, knowledge, and financial stability, they would undoubtedly answer with a resounding "Yes!" In fact, if I asked you and members of the Mafia about values, you would find that you both hold the same values near and dear to your hearts. Do members of the Mafia value family, freedom, creativity, collaboration, and honesty among their own? Of course, they do. Wait a minute. Am I suggesting we share many of the same values as the Mafia? Yes, that is what I am saying. It's not good, bad, right, or wrong. The Mafia has been highly effective in creating its organized crime syndicates. But just like any effective individual or company, the Mafia included, it isn't values that are moving the needle as far as progress is concerned. Check out the table below:

My Values	The Mafia's Values
Freedom	Freedom
Family	Family
Trust	Trust
Loyalty	Loyalty
Creativity	Creativity
Financial Stability	Financial Stability
Honesty	Honesty
Health	Health
Dependability	Dependability
Communication	Communication
Cooperation	Cooperation
Opportunity	Opportunity
Courage	Courage
Good Work Ethic	Good Work Ethic
Leisure Time	Leisure Time
Teamwork	Teamwork
Growth/Progress	Growth/Progress
Friendship	Friendship

The bottom line is that if you're human, with very few exceptions, you will inevitably share most of the same values as other humans. So, if you're single and looking for someone with the same values, you aren't doing yourself any favors because you aren't narrowing down the dating pool. And circling back to the company that goes on "values retreats," the values aren't necessarily going to move the needle as management intends.

My wife and I used to offer a powerful weekend seminar

called "Diabetes Smackdown." It was for people with type 2 diabetes and those at risk for developing it. Type 2 diabetes can be strongly influenced by lifestyle and diet, which makes it different from type 1 diabetes. The wonderful people who attended our seminars already knew to a large extent what they should be doing to manage their condition. They already knew they should exercise and choose different food to fuel their bodies. But they didn't understand *why* they could not follow through with the things they knew they should be doing and wanted to be doing to produce a better feeling outcome. When I asked the attendees, "Who values health and vitality?" they would all raise their hands. Again, we all value health and vitality. But simply valuing a state of being or an experience doesn't produce the desired result.

So what are values, and are they important? I invite you to consider that "Values are simply an indicator of preference." I'll say that again. "Values are simply an indicator of preference." And in that sense, they are important because they highlight what's important to us. They help inform us about ourselves. They indicate what we prefer. However, they do not determine the likelihood of achieving our desired outcome. We all prefer health and vitality, yet many contend with self-inflicted ill health. That was me for many years. We all prefer financial stability, yet most people don't have any significant financial safety net in the event of financial hardship. Again, that was me for many years. How about honesty? We prefer honesty, but let's face it, almost every one of us lies, whether it be an outright lie, a white lie, or an omission of information. It doesn't change the fact that we *prefer* honesty. But when it suits us, we will undoubtedly be willing to lie occasionally. And yes, that was definitely me for many years!

IF NOT VALUES, THEN WHAT DOES MOVE THE NEEDLE?

Ok, let's continue. If our values don't mean jack, where should our focus be? What should people look for in a partner? What should companies spend their time developing instead of core values? What will finally and most certainly move the needle in our health, wealth, and relationships? The answer is **standards.** Our standards determine the outcomes of our lives. Because "a standard is what you are willing to settle for." It's not necessarily what you want/prefer **(that's a value)** but instead what you are willing to settle for.

For years I was willing to settle for having a car payment. We would purchase a vehicle with very little down and *settle* for big monthly loan payments. Then we would trade in the car for a better one every few years and take on even bigger payments. It wasn't my preference to have a never-ending car payment. My preference was to own a car outright, free and clear. But my finances were such that we frequently juggled debt, and I thought everyone handled car ownership the way I was.

I'll never forget when a friend told me about the new truck he had just purchased. It was a nice big work truck, and I asked him what the monthly payments were. I was shocked when he told me he had no monthly payments. He paid cash for it! This blew my mind. How was that possible? Well, financial stability was not just a value for him and his wife but a standard. He told me that they set aside a certain amount of money every month into an auto fund. They would do this for years, and eventually, they would have enough money in their fund to purchase a car outright or at least make a significant down payment so they could pay off the vehicle quickly.

This may be what you already do when purchasing a new car, but for me, this was a new way of thinking about car ownership and managing my finances. I decided that I was going to do this as well. And at that moment, I changed my standard. I was no longer willing to settle for a never-ending car payment. My new standard was to implement my friend's methodology for saving. And it worked! We began buying our cars outright or would save enough for a significant down payment to allow a payoff in 12 to 18 months. But, we were no longer willing to settle for years of car payments.

At times, we may feel shocked and a bit ashamed to see what we have been willing to settle for. But, I encourage you to take that hard look to identify the standards that haven't served you. It's part of growing and a wonderful opportunity to create new standards. You see, most of our standards we didn't intentionally choose. Examples include our standards around eating, exercise, communication, finances, and choosing a partner. Even how you load the dishwasher likely wasn't consciously chosen by you.

And though we clearly did not choose all of our standards, we are ultimately responsible for the outcomes we produce as a result. Still, it can be hard to swallow when we realize that much of our suffering in life is because we have been willing to settle for situations or experiences that haven't served us. We've been willing to settle for living paycheck to paycheck. We've been willing to stay quiet instead of asking for a raise or figuring out how to bring more value to the workplace. Sometimes it shows up in our relationships. We are willing to settle for a lack of connection, authenticity, and intimacy. Getting honest with ourselves about our standards is one of the most powerful conversations we can have. When we get honest with ourselves, it's an opportunity to create a lasting transformation.

I have the utmost respect for the attendees at the Diabetes Smackdown. Many had suffered severe depression, been on various medications, and "tried everything." Some had or were facing amputation or at risk for blindness. I admire them because instead of throwing in the towel, they showed up ready to ask tough questions and learn something new about themselves. Personal development seminars can be uncomfortable and flat-out unsettling. It's frequently a vulnerable experience if you are open to it. And the result of being vulnerable and efforting through serious self-inquiry is gaining access to growth, progress, and new results.

IS IT TIME TO SET A NEW STANDARD?

There comes a point in our seminar and my coaching curriculum when we discuss the cost of our standards. What have our standards cost us regarding our health, finances, relationships, and how we see ourselves? We get clear on the impact that our standards have had. Then the fun begins! Once we identify a standard that doesn't serve us, we create a new one that feels good and will serve us.

I'll never forget three women who attended one of our Diabetes Smackdown seminars. They radically changed their standards. They were no longer willing to settle for lifelong medications, feeling depressed and fueling their bodies with foods that didn't serve them. They all enrolled in my coaching curriculum and began transforming their mindsets. And, while working through The

Practice of Feeling Good, they decided to challenge themselves by signing up for their first-ever triathlon. This was a commitment that required courage.

Within a year, all three lowered their medications or came off some of them entirely. They blew the minds of their physicians. Their depression lifted. They were feeling engaged in life, happy, and fulfilled because they were experiencing massive progress. Progress always feels good. I watched joyfully as these women persevered through emotional doubts and physical discomfort to cross the finish line to the cheers of family and friends. There were lots of tears, smiles, and high-fives. It was a spectacular moment. And I should mention that two of these women were in their 60s, and one was 70! They had successfully created new standards. And they had a new view of what was possible. They were able to experience a new level of vitality because standards produce results. And when your standards align with your values, you experience incredible momentum!

In my personal life, I have always valued financial stability. However, if you had looked at my checking account many years ago, you would have seen that I was living paycheck to paycheck and accruing overdraft fees. So even though I valued financial stability, the standard I was willing to settle for was living paycheck to paycheck and being unable to pay all my bills on time or in full. At some point, I set a new financial standard. Looking at my account now, you will see that I maintain a significant buffer. My new standard is always to have more than I need in the account just in case I make an accounting mistake or in case there is a small, unplanned expense.

Remember the earlier story about my triathlons? If you had asked me 20 years ago if I valued health and fitness, I would have said, "Absolutely." But was I doing anything productive in that particular area of my life? No. I was making poor food choices, and I wasn't intentionally exercising. I just thought, "Hey, I'm thin, so I must be healthy." At a certain point in my mid to late twenties, I started to experience a lot of discomfort in my joints and developed arthritis. I didn't attribute it to my diet or lack of intentional caring for my body. I just knew that exercising didn't feel good. It hurt. I settled on the notion that it must be "bad genes." And I used that story to defend my decision not to exercise.

My friends had other ideas for me, though. For years, they invited me to participate in triathlons with them. I had a limiting belief that triathlons were only for elite athletes. But I started to examine my standards. My chronic arthritis was not serving my life. I was young and wanted more of that abundant energy that my friends seemed to have. My friends were so gracious. They were willing to meet me at my level and help push me through the training. Sure, I couldn't bike long distances at first. And the most swimming experience I had was jumping off a dock, splashing around for a few seconds, and scrambling back to the shore. But I started training and took baby steps. I began creating health and fitness. I dealt with my body's discomfort, which began to lessen as I became stronger. Eight months later, I entered my first triathlon. I completed it and felt proud! I had successfully produced a feel-good outcome by raising my standard. When you change your standard, things may not happen right away. It might take many months or even longer to meet this new standard. But, once you declare it, you create an opportunity to live into it.

Keep in mind we have been discussing raising our standards. But, it's important to mention that sometimes it makes sense to lower our standards. To be clear, our standards are not good or bad. I have had an interesting conversation with myself over the past few years about my level of fitness. I had to ask myself: "Does maintaining this high level of fitness serve my life?" It served my life for a while, but given the time commitment required to maintain that fitness level, I decided to lower my standard intentionally. This is encouraged! There is nothing wrong with changing your standards. Life's a journey; it is not a fixed experience. And all that matters is that your standards are serving your life. Today, my goal is to be able to complete the distances of a sprint triathlon any day of the week. This standard requires me to maintain a certain level of fitness without consuming my entire life. Knowing what I'm willing to settle for regarding health and fitness feels good.

Now please hear this. There's nothing good, bad, right, or wrong about having type 2 diabetes, living paycheck to paycheck, having a car payment, or having a drink or two multiple nights a week. But it's imperative to ask, "What is my standard around this area of my life or particular behavior? Does this standard serve my life?" And if you decide that it doesn't serve you, there is an opportunity to set a new standard. Our standards impact every aspect of our lives.

A FEEL-GOOD TIP

I've learned that the fastest way to raise my standards to produce new and desired outcomes is to be around people with the standards and outcomes I want. When I increased my fitness and health, I began hanging out with others who already had outstanding outcomes in that area of their lives. When I decided to raise my financial standards, I surrounded myself with people who had done what I wanted to do because of those high standards. Many of the people I surrounded myself with were in the courses I took. I began consuming books, CDs, and online content. If you don't have access to people in your local area, then go online. Free and pay-to-play content is abundant. But know that your standards will usually be very close to those you hang out with regularly. For some of us, we may need to create new relationships.

As we end this chapter, I want to remind you that your values don't mean jack. They are indicators of preference. If you want to move the needle in any area of your life, take a good look at your standards. If you get honest with yourself and acknowledge what you've been willing to settle for, you allow yourself the opportunity to raise or lower the standard to produce a new, exciting result. Go for it!

Key Takeaways

- A value is an indicator of preference. Values *don't* move the needle or produce outcomes.
- With few exceptions, people share the same values.
- Standards are what we are willing to settle for. Our standards are responsible for the outcomes we produce.
- The fastest way to effectively create a new standard is to get around people who already have the standard you desire.

Opportunity to Practice

1. Do you value a clean and organized car? Yes/No
   a. What has been your standard for how you keep your car?
      i. Messy/Dirty/Cluttered
      ii. Clean, organized, and feels good when you get into it.

2. Do you value a clean and organized house/apartment? Yes/No
   a. What has been your standard for how you keep your living space?
      i. Messy/Dirty/Cluttered
      ii. Clean, organized, and feels good when you come home.

3. Do you value health and fitness? Yes/No
   a. Do you have clear standards around your health and fitness? Yes/No
   b. What have you been willing to settle for in your health? Be honest and specific.
   c. Is it time to raise your standards? If so, what do you want your new standards to be? (**Feel-good tip**: Take baby steps. Set yourself up for success. Instead of going from 0-60, try going from 0-1 or 0-5). Progress over perfection!

4. Do you value financial stability? Yes/No
   a. Do you have clear standards around how you save and spend money? In other words, can you easily articulate

to another person how you save and spend in a manner that is consistent with your desired outcomes?

5. Do you value family time? Yes/No
   a. Do you have a clear standard for family time? Yes/No
   b. What is your standard? Examples: You all eat dinner together four times a week. You have set times for board games weekly/monthly. You take regular vacations together as a family.

6. Want to really go for it? Here is some extra credit. Go through the table below.

Value/Preference	Standard
I value/prefer ongoing personal growth.	What standards do you have in place or want to create?
I value/prefer annual vacations.	What standards do you have in place or want to create?
I value/prefer a clean kitchen.	What standards do you have in place or want to create?
I value/prefer contribution.	What standards do you have in place or want to create?
I value/prefer date nights with my partner.	What standards do you have in place or want to create?
I value/prefer healthy communication.	What standards do you have in place or want to create?
I value/prefer a thriving community.	What standards do you have in place or want to create?
I value/prefer a thriving planet.	What standards do you have in place or want to create?

7

GRATITUDE

"Joy springs from a grateful heart."
- Fletcher Ellingson

The number one thing we want in life is to feel good. Gratitude is a foundational piece to creating a feel-good life. Before we continue, let's take a moment to create a working definition of gratitude and clarify how I am using this term. There are lots of definitions for gratitude. My best understanding of gratitude is an authentic acknowledgment and appreciation of something you cannot take credit for.

Practicing gratitude will magnify and intensify your experiences. I will share one of my favorite examples- Maui! My wife and I make it a priority to travel to Maui every year. I've never been to a place that feels as good as Maui. I feel enthusiastic, relaxed, inspired, connected, and present when I'm there. I'm moved by this island and feel deeply grateful for it. I enjoy getting up early to watch the sunrise. I usually go for a walking meditation, where I list all the things for which I'm grateful. I practice voicing my gratitude out loud. It may sound odd to some to start spouting off gratitudes. But that's what I do. I walk and talk to myself. I'm grateful for the sand, the ocean, the rainbows, the jungles, the turtles, and all the ocean life. I'm grateful for the Hawaiian people and the "aloha" spirit. I'm grateful for the sunsets, sunrises, the bright stars at night, and the ever-present warm wind. I'll continue expressing this way until I feel finished.

As a result, I feel even more connected, present, and filled up. If you refer to my Maui list of gratitude, it's easy to see I can't take credit for any of those items I say out loud on the beach. All of the universal forces that went into making Maui what it is took place without me. I have nothing to do with any of it. In gratitude, we acknowledge that which feels good. I don't mean good as a moral judgment. Maui, for instance, is neither good nor bad. But in the context of this practice, I experience it as beautiful and feel-good.

Gratitude is a beautiful practice, it's *easy* and free, and we can do it often! A critical part of The Practice of Feeling Good is practicing this way of being called "grateful." Remember, in the Cycle of Six, our ways of being influence our actions which determine our results and outcomes. So, you can imagine how sitting in gratitude would affect your actions and, therefore, your results. Would you be less likely or more likely to feel present and connected with loved ones after walking on the beach and filling yourself up with gratitude? Would you have more energy or less energy? Would you be more or less likely to see things working well?

My wife and I live in Chelan, Washington. It's at the base of a 50-mile-long, stunningly beautiful lake called Lake Chelan. It is a small town of about 5,000 year-round residents and one of the most breathtaking areas in our country. We frequently go to the big city of Wenatchee, which is a town of about 50,000 people. It's just shy of a 60-minute drive. One of the things we enjoy doing to pass the time during our ride to Wenatchee is to share out loud what we feel grateful for at that moment. What I love about this practice is that I feel good when I express my gratitudes, and I also feel good listening to my wife share her gratitudes. It's a double dose of good.

Again, this is a practice, and implementing it can initially feel odd. We're not used to noticing the good in the world and talking about it with people. In fact, most people are practiced at the exact opposite. We've been trained to notice what's not working and where others are falling short. And it's completely acceptable and commonplace to share all of that with others. We have mastered complaining, blame, and victimization, all putting us into a suffering state of mind.

Gratitude can also be a healing and restorative balm. When we are in a suffering state of mind, the number one thing we can do to interrupt the suffering program is to focus on gratitude. Doing so can ease anxiety, worry, and insecurity. What you focus on, you feel. If you're acknowledging good in the world and appreciating it, your brain has to create an emotional experience to go along with your focus. You diminish your suffering by focusing on gratitude. If you do this even for a couple of minutes, you can start to exit suffering and enter into a feel-good state of mind where you have access to progress.

ACKNOWLEDGMENT AND APPRECIATION

Practicing gratitude interrupts the pattern of obsessing about the future or the past. It brings us into the present moment. We are present and acknowledging "what is" without expecting the subject for which we are grateful to be other than it is. There is a flavor of enthusiastic receiving, experiencing, and embracing of "what is" when I acknowledge the sand, the ocean, the sky, etc. I'm present to it. I feel connected to it. I experience, receive, and embrace it. It feels good. And it's about to get even better. Read on...

Earlier, I said there is acknowledgment and appreciation in gratitude. I love the concept of appreciation. What does it mean for something to appreciate? It means the value of that thing increases. It could be a person, place, item, or experience. For instance, one of the primary reasons people invest in real estate is because they count on the high probability that the real estate will increase in value or appreciate. But let's get curious about what causes something to appreciate. If we look at the real estate example, we might be tempted to say that a house appreciates when we fix it up or make improvements. That sounds logical, right? We invested money into it, so it has to be worth more. It sounds logical, but it's not necessarily accurate. Let me explain.

Home prices fluctuate. But when they appreciate or depreciate, it's only for one reason. It is worth more or less simply because we say so. We speak value into existence. And then, we get the agreement of others; we gather consensus.

What do I mean by this? If you look to rent or purchase a home, you'll know that the people presenting the home will offer a long list of all its wonderful features. The list establishes a higher perception of value in your mind. You have a list of amenities and features to focus on, become present to, and begin to feel connected with. You begin to appreciate the colors of the paint. You run your hand over the smooth counters in the kitchen; you notice how good all the natural light feels coming in through the living room windows. And as you begin to talk about these things, you focus more and more on them. And remember what you focus on, you feel. So you begin to feel good, optimistic, hopeful, and eager. You begin to envision your furniture in the dining room and living room. You imagine having coffee or tea in the morning while looking out those big picture windows or staring out at the night sky from the private deck. The value of the home begins to increase in your mind. The concept of appreciation is profound because it is all occurring in language. Language weaves a story to which we then attach a value.

Take a moment and consider what the extraordinary applications of this are. This means you can increase anything's value simply by verbalizing your appreciation of it. It may be sentimental or financial value, practical or emotional value, or even spiritual value. But one of the most powerful uses of appreciation is to increase the value of people. It's like having a magic wand. We can increase people's value in our minds by simply acknowledging and looking for things to appreciate about them.

I invite you to imagine doing this regularly about those closest to us. What would happen if we began to focus on all the fantastic things we could find about an individual? We would start to experience a greater affinity for that person. They would become more valuable to us. Imagine if that person is your spouse, one of your parents, a sibling, or a child.

Imagine if that person you are appreciating is *you*. That's right; you can increase your self-worth simply by practicing self-appreciation. Isn't there so much to appreciate about yourself? You've put in so much effort. You've done your best in light of all of your current programming. You know your heart; you want to be loved and give love. You want to make a difference. Appreciate all those things about yourself. You work hard. At times you go the extra mile. You're kind, want goodness in the world, and are working on becoming the next best version of yourself. You're open to growth. Remind yourself of all of this. Say it out loud. You'll feel present, you'll feel connected, and it will feel good and fill you up.

I frequently appreciate things and people in my mind as well as saying it out loud. But it's even more potent when we take the opportunity to appreciate someone to their face. Why? Because not only are we increasing their value in our mind, but we create an opportunity for the other person to receive the appreciation and therefore experience an increase in their self-worth. It's extraordinary and can be a beautiful, feel-good gift. It reminds me of one of my favorite quotes:

> *"I've learned that people will forget what you said, people will forget what you did, but people will never forget how you **made them feel**." - Maya Angelou*

THE JOY/GRATITUDE CONNECTION

I invite you to play around with gratitude. Share your gratitude with others. Ask others what they're grateful for, or ask people what's going well in their life. It's a different and beautiful way to connect with people. It interrupts their patterns and allows for a unique, refreshing conversation. If you want to experience more joy in your life, not just happiness, but joy, then focus on gratitude. Joy springs from a grateful heart.

Think of all the times we feel joy. The birth of a baby and watching that baby grow and develop brings a sense of joy.

Celebrating a marriage is frequently a joyous occasion. If you pay attention, you'll see that what precedes joy is gratitude. Next time you watch the Oscars or any awards banquet, listen carefully to the language used. What you'll frequently see is that the recipient is full of gratitude. They often acknowledge and appreciate the people who helped them accomplish what they are being recognized for. They acknowledge and appreciate the good for which they cannot take credit. They feel connected, present, and filled up. Gratitude is magical.

Key Takeaways

- Gratitude is an authentic acknowledgment and appreciation of something good for which you cannot take credit.
- Practicing gratitude interrupts the pattern of obsessing about the future or the past. It brings us into the present moment, where life is actually occurring.
- Focusing on gratitude diminishes worry and anxiety and is the fastest way out of a suffering mindset.
- Gratitude is access to experiencing more joy.

Opportunity to Practice

1. On a scale of one to ten, with ten being the highest, how grateful do you feel on a daily basis? Write this down in your journal.
2. Where would you like to experience more gratitude and joy in your life? Identify at least three areas.

3. Make a list of ten things for which you can be grateful for right now.
    a. BONUS: Intensify your gratitude by appreciating those things on your list, meaning talk about why you are grateful for them. What's great about them?
4. Identify someone you feel safe with and can share your gratitudes with. Invite them to do the same with you.

Feel-Good Tip: Set two or three alarms on your phone to go off during the day. Use them as a reminder to become present and practice being grateful.

8

HOW TO TRANSFORM RESENTMENT

Peace is a big concept, and people use the word peace to mean many different things. People frequently tell me they want to experience more peace in their life. When they talk about it, they're not talking about peace between nations. They mean they want a personal, emotional experience of peace. And when I ask them to define peace, they struggle with it.

They usually don't have many descriptors to define what peace actually is. But they do have descriptors for what peace is not. They're clear about what they don't want to feel. They don't want to feel stressed, anxious, fearful, upset, angry, agitated, frustrated, jealous, guilty, ashamed, inadequate, or insecure. You can see how telltale this answer is; we put more energy into noticing what doesn't feel good. We're tuned in and practiced at noticing what isn't working, who's falling short, and hyper-aware of how we're missing the mark. We obsessively practice not feeling good and notice what doesn't feel good in the world.

It's easy to understand why so many people say they want peace. They don't have it because they're focusing on the opposite of it. And we know what we focus on, we feel. What we focus on expands and becomes our point of attraction. This means when we're practiced at noticing what doesn't feel good, we inevitably get more of it; we set ourselves up for feeling worse.

Creating thoughts requires energy. So understand that you are directing energy to create thoughts that don't feel good and don't serve you. If someone asked you to allocate a large percentage of your energy toward thoughts that don't feel good and would turn into words, actions, and eventually outcomes that don't serve you, you would find that to be a crazy request. Yet, we frequently do precisely that - use our precious energy to create stories that don't serve us.

The Practice of Feeling Good is about intentionally focusing your energy on thinking feel-good thoughts and speaking them into the physical space so they expand and ultimately manifest. You turn your thoughts into matter by bringing energy to them. There's a saying I have heard over the years that addresses this, "We matterize that which matters to us." Every thought and story is created with energy. The more you focus on a thought, the more energy you give it, and the more likely it is to *matterize*. And the brain doesn't care whether or not the thought serves you. It has no choice but to get into emotional alignment.

Let's revisit the initial concept of peace. When people tell me they want peace in their lives, they mean they want the people and the situations around them to be more peaceful. They want people to be kind, accepting, and open. They want people and situations to align with the fantasy in their minds. Most people's ability to experience peace is conditional and almost entirely dependent on the actions of those around them. This condition is the perfect breeding ground for resentment. And resentment kills our ability to experience any level of inner peace.

RESENTMENT

Many of us are masterfully practiced at resenting. We have decades of practice resenting people we feel wronged us somehow. I used to resent previous business partners, neighborhood bullies, teachers, family members, politicians, governments, religions, media, and certain corporations. I had a lot of resentments. When we're honest with ourselves, we'll see that resentments permeate our lives, and there cannot be any meaningful peace while we're holding on to them.

Let's define resentment. There are several definitions, but my best understanding is that *resentment is a multi-layered, resistance-based story resulting in an intensely judgmental and disempowering reaction.* Notice the keyword in that last statement: **story**. Remember the question I asked earlier about fear and courage? What is at the center of fear and courage? The answer is a story. It works the same way here. At the center of resentment is a powerful story that causes massive suffering, destruction, and devastation to our relationships and lives.

So what do the stories of resentment look and sound like? Well, they usually center around the idea that we were wronged. Somehow, we felt taken advantage of or like someone embarrassed or shamed us, making us look bad in some way. We may believe we were wrongly or falsely accused. Maybe someone stole from us. Or we might feel that one of our rights has been violated. Perhaps someone close to us had an affair that resulted in pain and impacted our lives. The frequent emotions that travel with resentment are indignation, disgust, helplessness, fear, repulsion, anger, jealousy, righteousness, and the desire for punishment and justice.

As I mentioned, it's a multi-layered emotional experience. This colossal upset does not feel good, and when we are in it and feeling terrible, we want out of it. For most people, the logical explanation is that someone else needs to change so we can feel better. The person who caused our suffering could end it if they changed, stopped being so unfair, or ceased being rude and inconsiderate. We could feel better if justice was served, if they got what was coming to them, were arrested, punished, or lost financially or relationally. If they suffered some major karmic misfortune, we could begin feeling peace.

Resentment is not pretty. It's ugly and destructive, and we cannot have peace as long as we are resentful. So what has been the cost of your resentment? I believe my intense resentment at times in my life contributed to significant inflammation in my body, resulting in various physical discomforts. I think that it impacted my ability to sleep at night. And that lack of sleep exacerbated my inflammation. At times I entertained taking actions that would have landed me in jail. I was angry, and my upset spilled out on those close to me. I had a sense of helplessness. My thoughts were consumed by how I was wronged and my desire for punishment and "justice." I wanted the people and situation to change so I could feel good again. I would go to bed resenting, and I would wake up resenting. I was caught in a loop and didn't know how to put an end to the crazy ride.

RESISTANCE

Can you relate to any of this? If so, you know how terrible it feels. What, then, can we do about it? How can we interrupt this program and begin to create peace? Peace. There's that word again.

It sounds so simple, so easy. Yet, why does it feel so out of reach, and why do most of us experience so little of it? Because we're practiced at the opposite of it. What's the opposite of peace? Some people will say war. But war is a symptomatic result of practicing the opposite of peace. The opposite of peace is **resistance**. Resistance is at the core of all of our suffering. We're so practiced at resisting that there's no room for peace. Am I being dramatic? I don't think so. Consider the following.

We resist our husband or wife; we want them to think and act differently than they do. We want our children to think and act differently than they do. We want drivers on the road to be driving other than how they are driving. They should travel faster, slower, or not so close to us. They should be safer or not on the road at all. Resistance really shows up on the road. We also resist teachers, the government, clients, and parents. We wish they would talk differently to us, hear us differently, and act differently. Consider all the times in your day when you feel irked, a lot or even a little, because something happens that you think should have happened differently. That is resistance.

What's at the center of resistance? There's that question again. You got it. A story. In this case, it's a story that someone should be other than they are or something should be other than it is; ultimately, life should be other than it is. And you can see how that can make us feel crazy. We are resisting "what is." We're such incredibly sophisticated beings, yet we regularly resist reality. We expect people to be other than they are. We expect their programming to be different. We expect life to be different. The weather should be different. They don't love me the right way. They shouldn't get a divorce; they shouldn't get married; they should be going to college; they should be doing more with their life; they should be paying me more; they should have given me the promotion. They shouldn't have been elected. I should have more money; things should be more manageable. There isn't enough time. Yes, we even resist time. It's kind of comical when you stop and think about it.

When we resist, we break from reality and are pulled out of the present moment. What I mean by that is we go into our fantasy world where the people in our life show up differently. In this alternate universe, they think and behave in a manner that aligns with what we want. *They're less like themselves and more of who we want them to be.* Ouch! When we really get the weight of that last statement, we can see how problematic that thinking is.

Resistance doesn't feel good. It's like playing the wrong chords in a song on the piano. You can physically feel the dissonance; you feel it in your body because you can feel vibrations. Everything, at its essence, is a form of vibration, including resistance. And, when you get present to how resistance feels in your body and your emotions, you will feel that dissonance.

THE ANTIDOTE TO RESISTANCE IS IN NEW DECISIONS

We are masters of resisting, which then breeds resentment, which then has the potential to devastate our lives. So how do we best handle resistance and resentment? Dealing with our resistance to life requires two powerful decisions.

Decision one: "I am deciding to surrender my resentments of people in my life." Wow, that's a powerful decision that flies in the face of what we have been doing. Previously, we thought it was okay to resent people. It was okay to expect them to be other than they were. We felt they deserved our resentment. We thought we were right. In the first decision, we are surrendering that expectation. To me, surrendering means releasing that which doesn't serve my life. So we are deciding to release our expectation that people should be other than who they are. We release our expectation that life should show up differently than it is. This is powerful and, of course, will take a lot of deliberate practice. I want to make this practice a bit easier by suggesting another decision.

The second decision is a radical concept. So it's best to hear this from a place of openness. Take a moment to get open. Close your eyes and take a couple of deep breaths before reading on. Resenting people and thinking people should be doing better than they are has poisoned us. It's taken a toll on our relationships, finances, health, and the ability to create our lives powerfully. We've been focusing on inaccurate stories that have not served others or us. So in decision number two, we will make a declaration that may initially feel uncomfortable. Still, I encourage you to hang in there with me and trust this process because again and again, I see this simple decision create powerful changes in relationships and allow for healing, growth, and thriving.

Decision two: "I am deciding that everyone is always doing the best they can, given all their past experiences and their current programming." Read that again. Everyone is always doing their best. Now some people, upon hearing this, will object and tell me they are sure they know people in their life that are not doing the best they can. They tell me that they witness people lying and cheating. They tell me that people are not parenting their best. Politicians are not representing and leading as best they can. People are not driving their best, and on and on. I'm not saying people's best has integrity or doesn't cause harm. A person's best in some situations may even be unlawful. But it's still their best at that moment, given all of their programming. Their actions may not make sense to us. But then again, much of what we do may not make sense to others.

I know that's been the case in my life. When my 18-year marriage ended, that was me doing my best. At my best, I was not able to hold my marriage together. When I caused a head-on car collision, that was me doing my best. When I yelled and swore and threw things out of frustration, feeling at my wit's end, that was me doing my best. When I forgot birthdays and anniversaries, that was me doing my best. When I forgot to make a payment, yep, that was me at my best. When I didn't show up powerfully for myself and others, that was me at my best. Now, if you know me, you may think I'm a pretty high-caliber person. And I feel like I am. Yet at times, my best has not looked very good. In fact, it appeared broken and messy. If you know me, you may say, "Oh, yeah, Fletcher, but we all make mistakes. Don't be too hard on yourself."

That's my point. We all make mistakes- the person driving in front of you, your husband, wife, ex, kids, and in-laws. It may be hard to communicate with or get along with them sometimes. People may not make the choices you think they should make or say the things you think they should. But they're doing their best just like you. We all make mistakes as we navigate life. I make lots of mistakes. Think of how many mistakes you've made. How many lies have you told, or how many times have you omitted the truth or stolen or cheated? Have there been times you were the one driving too slowly or forgot to turn off your blinker? Have there been times you forgot the important date or were late for the meeting? Have there been times you were rude or mean, or uncaring? Were there times you knew what to do but didn't do it? Can you see that in those times, you, too, were doing your best to cope with life?

We are all struggling with feelings of insecurity and fear. It causes us to do things we're not proud of. It causes us to violate our morals. And the more desperate we feel, the more we're willing to do something that doesn't serve us or others. Look at Robin Williams. He was beloved by the world. And by most people's standards, he had incredible success. He had people who loved him, money, and a fulfilling career, and he made people laugh and cry. He made people feel good. And yet he ended his life. Isn't that wild to consider? Ending his life was him at his best. That was the best he could do at that moment. Only those close to him know the demons he was battling, but it's safe to say he was struggling, and ending his life was him doing his best.

It's time we realize that people have wide ranges of programming, and everyone is always doing their best, even if it doesn't look like it. It doesn't mean we have to condone people's actions. It doesn't mean there are no consequences. It doesn't mean we don't hold people accountable. It doesn't mean that we don't stand up for ourselves. But what it allows us to do is release our judgment. It's challenging to judge someone when we realize that they're doing their best. When we recognize and release our judgment, we suddenly have access to something that our world needs in a big way: compassion and empathy. This is the road to peace.

We're cut off from compassion and empathy as long as we judge others. And without compassion and empathy, there is no access to healing. People want to heal physically, emotionally, spiritually, and financially and feel united as a local and global community. But when resentment and judgment are present, we're cut off from healing because we don't have access to understanding, compassion, and empathy. We don't have to understand what happened to people and why they are doing what they're doing. But we can know that they're doing their best with the tools they have, their upbringing, their schooling or lack of schooling, their love or lack of love, and their opportunities or lack of opportunities. With all their crushing fears of rejection, failure, and not being good enough, humans are doing their best. I know I am. You may think, "Yeah, but I know people can do better." I caution you on immediately jumping to this conclusion. In fact, you can be sure that your programming is attempting to assert itself again with this thought. You see, they can't do any better than they are doing right now. Right now, they are at their best.

And yes, people can learn to do better in the future, especially when others reach out to them, care for them, believe in them, and are willing to release judgment and show kindness and compassion. When people experience kindness and feel heard and seen, they feel safe. And it is at this moment, when a person feels safe, that they can begin to do better. In this moment of feeling safe, we can start acting outside some of our programs. When we feel safe, we can be present instead of worrying about the future or regretting the past. We can take our programs off autopilot just long enough to see different opportunities and possibilities.

We understand that we resist, judge, and resent people at times. We also understand what we can do about it now. But what about when people resist us? What about when people judge or resent us? I've had plenty of people judge and resent me. It doesn't feel good to be on the receiving end of that. I got in trouble a lot while growing up. It was always a fearful experience for me. I didn't feel safe. I felt like I had severely disappointed people when they were upset with me. It's likely why I used to lie so much. I lied to avoid getting in trouble. My fear of "being in trouble" traveled well into adulthood. Maybe you can relate.

Wanting to break this cycle of fear, I began to ask: "Is there anything I can do about other people resenting me or being upset with me?" As a result of asking the question, my brain got to work. And it came up with a simple practice that, while uncomfortable, is effective. I can't force people to think or feel one way or the other about me, but I can create a space where they feel safe sharing with me authentically. I know that when I am resentful, it's because of a story I am focusing on, which is usually inaccurate, or I may not have all the facts.

I'll use my marriage as an example. When I am worried that my wife is unhappy with me or that I am in trouble, I ask her, "Does it feel like there is anything between us right now?" I love this question because it doesn't accuse anyone of anything. It simply creates a space that allows for someone to share.

It is important to create a safe space for authentic sharing. Sometimes I might say, "I am feeling insecure. Does it feel like there is anything between us?" The point is to take responsibility, avoid accusations, and provide an opening for sharing. This can feel scary to do. But remember, if you feel fearful, there is an opportunity to be courageous. Imagine how good it will feel to work things out and restore a sense of warmth and connection. You can use this method in any of your personal or work relationships; every time you do this, it will get easier. Now, let's bring it full circle.

FLOW

At the top of this chapter, I said people long for peace. What they mean is they want to experience a sense of flow. Flow is that magical spot where you have momentum, and things click and fall into place. In flow, you have access to progress. There is diminished resistance. You can access energy, healing, enthusiasm, and creativity. Flow and peace are much the same. One thing that gets in the way of both is resistance. Resistance is the killer of peace and flow. Earlier in this chapter, we learned that we frequently want and even expect the conditions around us to change so that we can feel better. But now we know that doesn't work. To experience peace, an absence of resistance, we must transform our story about people and life itself. Our opportunity is to surrender our judgment and get curious about people from a place of empathy and compassion. Our opportunity is to be a beacon of hope and kindness. **Our opportunity is to be a clearing for others to feel safe, heard, and empowered.**

Releasing resistance is a practice. It's the most challenging and essential practice because our resistance to life is the cause of our greatest suffering. The program of resistance is strong and is integrated into who we are. I don't know that we can fully extricate ourselves from this program. But we can interrupt the program more quickly and frequently, reducing our suffering.

I'll share one of my personal practices. When I see that my program of resistance has been triggered, I say to myself, "Oh, there goes my program again, running without my permission or approval." I notice the program is active. And when I notice it, I see that I am not the program. This is a big deal because sometimes we think we and the program are the same. But that is not the case. Seeing that I am not the program, I've created a bit of space between myself and it. And in that space, I can begin to act outside of the program. At this moment, I say the following mantra, "Hey there, universe, my program got triggered. I'm suffering and need help. I surrender my resistance and trust that life is always working out for my greatest evolution."

This simple act and these simple words feel good. Asking for help is a sign of strength. It diminishes the resistance and allows access to doing better. I return to an empowering story about people and life in general. Now, it may feel awkward at first, and that's okay. That's why it's called a practice. With practice, it will eventually become comfortable. I'll be practicing this for the rest of my life. And I've seen this practice heal marriages, business relationships, and friendships. I've been healed by it. If you are looking for healing, it can provide the healing you seek. Everything we need to experience peace is within us. Now, it all comes down to the practice.

Key Takeaways

- Resentment is a response to resisting people, situations, and life.
- Resistance is our greatest cause of suffering.
- People are always doing their best, given all of their current programming.
- Understanding people are doing their best allows for greater empathy and compassion.
- We can begin to interrupt resentments by asking, "Is there anything between us?"

Opportunity to Practice

1. What resentments are you holding onto? Are you resenting people, situations, institutions, policies, groups of people, or countries? Write down at least four examples.
2. What is the story at the center of this resentment? Does the story feel good? Does it serve you?
3. What has been the cost of these resentments?
4. Practice making two powerful decisions:
    a. I'm deciding to surrender my judgment of this person or situation.
    b. I'm deciding this person is doing the best they can, given all their past experiences and current programming.
5. Create a feel-good mantra like the one I described above. Keep this mantra close by and ideally memorize it. You can then say it when you realize you are stuck in resentment and resistance.

9

LIFE'S MAGIC WAND

"That living word awakened my soul, gave it light, hope, joy, set it free!"
- Helen Keller

I've been a performing magician for 35 years. While I enjoy entertaining people, I also really appreciate being fooled. That brief moment of witnessing something that defies logic and physics is such a wonderful treat. I love the experience of surprise and astonishment and not having any explanation for what just occurred. That moment is so rare for adults and is really the gift of magic.

One of the interesting things about magic is how a magician uses magically-infused words and phrases to create awe-inspiring feats. This directly correlates with how we create our lives. We'll get to that shortly. But first, we have to ask an important question about life. Where does our experience of life occur? That may seem like an odd question, but consider it for a moment. Where does our *experience of life* occur? You may think it happens right here, right now, where you are. Or you may think that it occurs everywhere you look. Perhaps you think that it occurs in your thoughts.

I invite you to consider that our experience of life occurs in relationships. I know this may sound odd, but think of all the people with whom we have relationships. We have parents, siblings, friends, spouses, romantic partners, co-workers, and acquaintances. We experience life to a large degree when interacting within those relationships. And those are just the "living relationships."

We also have relationships with people who have passed on. They are no longer here with us physically, and while the relationship has changed, it still exists. We think of them, talk to them, dream about them, and remember them. On top of that, consider the relationship you have with yourself. You are talking to yourself all day long. You make yourself laugh, get mad at yourself, are proud of yourself, and so on.

We also have relationships with others that are not even real. You can feel highly connected with the characters when you read a book or watch a TV show or movie. You may smile, laugh and cry as you interact with them. Have you ever finished a book or a TV series and longed to connect with those characters again? You may catch yourself wondering, "What are they doing now? How have they been?" You want to check in with them and spend time with them. They aren't even real, yet we have a relationship with them. It's why people may read a book or watch a movie more than once. We enjoy the relationships; we enjoy our experience of life with them.

Now your brain may be saying, "Well, what if all the people were suddenly gone from my life? What if I was on a remote island all by myself?" If that were the case, you would still be in relationship with yourself. You would also be in relationship with all sorts of things in your environment. There would be the trees, the sand, the rocks, the water, the life within the water, the sun, the wind, and the rain. Relationships are always happening around us and with us. Why do so many of us love to go out in nature? Because we feel deeply connected. We experience various emotions triggered by fresh and earthy scents, different designs and textures, and a broad spectrum of colors and sounds. And the other lovely experience in nature is that there's very little resistance. We are not judging the trees. We are not finding fault with them. We are not thinking, "That tree should be much taller and have more branches." No, we usually accept nature exactly as it is. It feels so good to accept things as they are.

We are always in relationship. Where are you right now? Are you sitting and reading this book? Then you're in a relationship with the chair you're sitting in. In fact, you're always making slight adjustments as you're sitting. You're adjusting your relationship with the chair. You may start to feel stiff or sore. So you adjust your posture, lean to one side or the other, and cross or uncross your legs. Your feet are in a relationship with the floor, shoes, and socks. As I type this, I'm in relationship with my keyboard. And even though we've never met, I'm in relationship with you as I think about you reading these words. You can see that our experience of life occurs in relationships.

Once we understand this concept, we get one step closer to a wonderful magic wand. And with this magic wand, you can begin to create your life powerfully. I'll explain more as we continue to explore this line of thinking. But first, here's another question. If our experience of life is occurring in relationship, then where does relationship occur? I know we're getting existential here, but we're heading somewhere important. Stay with me.

Where does relationship occur predominantly? Well, it occurs mainly in communication. There is nonverbal and verbal communication, but we will focus on the verbal. It's easy to see that relationships require communication. We express, engage, explore, and connect using verbal communication. We're all very proficient at this. We do it all day long, every day.

And now for a final question: Where does communication exist? Yes, you've got it - in language. **Language is the magic wand with which we create our experience.** Language allows us to create, express, and bring meaning to our world. Before Helen Keller knew language, there was a massive lack of knowing, understanding, certainty, and an inability to relate to her surroundings. However, upon learning to use language, she exclaimed, "The living word awakened my soul, gave it light, hope, joy, set it free!" Language transformed her relationship with everything around her and, thus, her experience of life. She used language to create her life, and wow, what a life she created! She was the first blind person to earn a bachelor's degree. She authored 12 books, became a social and political activist, a speaker, and even performed in vaudeville shows. Hellen Keller was recognized as one of the most influential people of the 20th century. Though she couldn't see, hear, or speak, she learned to use language to create her life.

We all use language to create. Language allows us to form thoughts, which are then communicated in the physical space and ultimately become things, events, and experiences. We create marriage and divorce through language. We raise our children through language. We declare war and peace through language.

We express our experiences of pain and pleasure through language. We use language to create and describe our past, present, and future experiences. In several religious texts, passages describe how God created the universe. How was it created? Language. Everything was spoken into existence.

ABRACADABRA

Remember that magic wand I mentioned? This is it. Language is our magic wand. One of the magic incantations we associate with magicians is "Abracadabra." I always thought it was just a nonsensical word that supposedly could cause a rabbit to appear out of a hat. The actual term "abracadabra" is a form of the Aramaic phrase "avra kehdabra," meaning "I will create as I speak."

Talk about powerful and magical - we create with our words. And isn't this accurate? Aren't we all creating with language? We declare who our friends are and who our enemies are using language. We create inventions, opportunities, and possibilities through language. When we say we can't do something, we experience the inability to do that thing. When we say, "I'm not good enough," we experience the sense of not being good enough. When we say there's never enough time or money, we experience a lack of both. When we're up against a challenge and say, "This is impossible," we experience the impossibility of the situation and feel defeated. But when we say, "I'm resourceful, capable, and flexible," we find a way to move beyond the challenge. When we say, "Money is abundant," we begin to attract more of it. When we say there are new clients out there heading our way, we see clients showing up. When we say we'll learn a new skill, start that business, or attract love, the ball starts rolling because we've spoken it into existence with our magic wand.

Unfortunately, we all too often use this powerful tool to our detriment. We've been saying people are jerks, can't be trusted, and life isn't working out for us. And so life corresponds with those words, and that's precisely what we experience. Many of us have suffered so much in life because we've been speaking suffering into existence. We've been doing this for so long that we've become masterfully practiced. It has become habitual to the point we don't even notice we're doing it. Then we wonder why so many things that don't feel good are happening to us. I'm not saying that challenging things will not happen to us. They will. Nor am I saying that all suffering results from language. Of course, we may find ourselves in physically and emotionally painful situations. And I assert that language can either intensify our suffering or help transform the situation so that we can evolve through the challenge.

EMPOWERING STORIES EXIST IN LANGUAGE

The Practice of Feeling Good is the practice of bringing an empowering story to any situation. The feel-good story exists in language. This is the new practice we want to master. When a challenge presents itself, instead of getting stuck in complaining or expressing our inadequacies, we can remind ourselves that we are powerful and resourceful. We can ask for help, seek the lesson, and grow through the challenge.

In 1979 Rotary International came up with the idea of eliminating polio worldwide. They spoke it into existence, and they promptly got to work. In 1988 they became a founding member of the Global Polio Eradication Initiative. Today, along with their partners, they have vaccinated over 2.5 billion children. This all happened because someone had the idea and spoke it into being.

On May 25th, 1961, John F. Kennedy and his administration declared they would send a rocket to the moon without knowing how it could even be accomplished. Eight years later, in July of 1969, the world witnessed the first-ever moon landing. That which was thought to be impossible by many was made possible because it was first an idea (in language) and then declared (in language).

My wife started a charitable organization to raise money to support sick and orphaned babies in Lesotho, Africa. She and a small group of dedicated friends used language to communicate their message to our community. This group then went on to have fundraising events for 15 years, raising hundreds of thousands of dollars. That financial support helped save children's lives and get them back to a place of thriving. This group initially started with the intention to make a difference for vulnerable children on the planet, and through language, the idea solidified into reality.

You may have heard the name Roger Bannister. He is famous in the world of running because he broke the four-minute mile. At the time, it was said to be impossible. In fact, many people thought a person would actually die if they attempted to do so; they believed the heart would burst or simply give out.

A name you may have yet to hear is John Landy. He was also a famous runner at the same time as Roger Bannister. But here's what he said about the four-minute mile. "Frankly, I think the four-minute mile is beyond my capabilities. Two seconds may not sound like much, but to me, it's like trying to break through a brick wall. Someone may achieve the four-minute mile. The world desperately wants it, but I don't think I can."

John Landy said it was impossible, so he didn't do it (at least not right away.) Roger Bannister felt differently about the four-minute mile and was the first person in the world to break it. His thinking and language were different from Landy's, so he did what everyone else said was impossible. However, after seeing Roger Bannister do it, John Landy changed his belief about what was possible. And, forty-six days after Roger Bannister had done the impossible, John Landy also broke the four-minute mile and even broke the record that Bannister had just set. Today, of course, thousands of people have broken the four-minute mile. These are all examples of language making the impossible... possible!

We use language to create the big and little things, the wins and losses, the pain and pleasure. It is all created and magnified or diminished through language. So now it's all up to you. What do you want to begin creating? Have fun with it. Abracadabra!

Key Takeaways

- Relationships occur in communication.
- Communication occurs predominantly in language.
- Language is the magic wand through which we create our life.
- Language allows for the impossible to become possible.

Opportunity to Practice

1. What have you created through language that has not served your life? List at least five examples.
2. What have you created through language that has served your life? List at least five examples.
3. Since you now know that you create your life with language, what do you want to begin to speak into existence? (More fun, wealth, health, fitness, healing, a vacation, a promotion, a loving relationship, an adventure, writing a book?) Make a list of at least three new things.

—10—
PUTTING IT ALL INTO PRACTICE

"Practice is access to progress."
- Fletcher Ellingson

We have become well-practiced at feeling insecure, upset, inadequate, depressed, indecisive, overwhelmed, offended, anxious, angry, and frustrated. On some level, we know that these ways of being don't serve us and can't sustain us. Sometimes when I am outside washing my car, the hose gets a big kink, and suddenly the water slows to a trickle. The flow is no longer adequate for the job at hand. A similar situation occurs when we are operating from a suffering state of mind. Our thoughts become all twisted up. The energy is directed toward thoughts and actions that don't serve us or those around us. It's like a big kink in the energetic hose, and our access to progress and growth is significantly impeded. As a result, life occurs to us as a struggle instead of an opportunity and blessing. We've lived like this for so long that it seems normal.

We have grown accustomed to suffering and struggle. We even expect it.

But we now know there is a different way of living. We have the option to live from a feel-good state of mind. And in that state, we have access to gratitude, joy, connection, growth, understanding, acceptance, contribution, creativity, and progress. Yes, it will take a commitment to practice intentionally. But practice is access to progress. When we commit to The Practice of Feeling Good, our relationships with others and ourselves transform for the better. We understand and appreciate that everyone is doing their best with the tools and programming they have. In this chapter, I will offer suggestions to help with the practice. Many of the tips derive from what I personally do on a regular basis. This is where the rubber meets the road. Join me!

A TRILOGY OF POWERFUL DECISIONS

Making powerful decisions is part of the practice. I have created three short audio recordings, "A Trilogy of Powerful Decisions," to help you practice. Each of them is about 3 or 4 minutes long. They will guide you through a meditative practice around trust, acceptance, and letting your light shine. Email me at fletcher@fletcherellingson.com and reference the Trilogy of Powerful Decisions, and I'll send them to you. You can listen to them in the morning to help you start your day with a feel-good state of mind. Or listen in the car or whenever you want to bring positive intention to your day.

THE "BEING OPEN" PRACTICE

This has been an extremely valuable exercise for me and is one of my favorites. It's easy to do and only takes a few minutes. I usually do this in the morning. I put on some pleasant music (no lyrics), sit for 3 to 10 minutes, and repeat the following statement: "I am open to_____" (and then I fill in the blank). Sometimes I intentionally fill in the blank, and sometimes I see what shows up. At the start of this practice, you may find yourself running out of things to be open to. But the more you do it, the more you will find. It's quite remarkable.

I'll give you some examples. Note that when I am actually doing the exercise, I enjoy using the "I am open to" phrase before each example. The repetition of "I am open" is valuable and what we want to emphasize. "I am open to…this moment, pain, healing, health, prosperity, mobility, the obstacle, solutions, helping, contributing, receiving, the weather, my friends, my partner, learning, making mistakes, taking risks, different perspectives, growth, laughter, lightheartedness, feedback, yes, no, fear, courage, listening, vulnerability, honesty, new relationships, acceptance, my life." While these examples are a bit general, I encourage you to get specific. Get clear on the things and situations you would like to be open to.

This has become an essential practice for me. It feels good to be open to life. In doing this, I have come to see that I have been closed to so much. It's exciting to become more and more open. I am open to the things I want and don't want. If a situation doesn't go my way, I am now more open to it and, therefore, can navigate it with greater ease.

For example, let's say you have had an important meeting planned for several weeks. You're excited about the potential outcome, and the day finally arrives. However, minutes before the meeting is supposed to take place, you get a phone call, and the meeting is called off. It isn't even rescheduled; just called off altogether with no explanation. This could feel like a major setback. And yes, it will feel disappointing, but now you are practicing being open to these situations. You can be open to the meeting being canceled. You can be open to a change of plans. You can be open to a flat tire, a delayed flight, or an unexpected bill. You can be open to how life shows up, even if it's not what you want. Being open instead of resisting significantly affects the quality of life. I will be the first to admit this takes practice. But you will notice a difference quickly. This practice is key to reducing suffering and navigating life more easily and joyfully. **Keep practicing being open.**

GRATITUDE

This is always a great place to begin. Sometimes we are in a state of suffering, so getting to "open" can be a giant leap. Going to gratitude can be a more accessible place to start. There is so much for which to be grateful. If, at first, it feels challenging, start with your body. You can be grateful for your sight and ability to hear, feel, and speak. Appreciate all your body does for you without your knowledge or involvement. You can be grateful for your mobility and your overall health. You can be grateful for oxygen, water, food, connection, opportunities, possibilities, transportation, and education. You can be grateful for the money in your bank account and the money on its way. You can be grateful for the weather, the roads you drive on, the stocked grocery stores, access to health care, and so on.

Expressing gratitude is always a grounding exercise. And if you want more joy in life, definitely focus on gratitude. Joy springs from gratitude. My wife and I frequently do "rounds" of gratitude. We'll do them in the car when we have a long drive. Or we'll do them when sitting by the ocean or sometimes at the end of a busy and stressful day.

You may want to journal your gratitude as another way to express it. But verbalizing it out loud is powerful. You engage your brain in a different way. Some element of vulnerability and connection is present when we vocalize our gratitude. What can you be grateful for? **Keep practicing gratitude.**

CONTRIBUTION

This is a wonderful opportunity to feel good and create access to connection and growth. Contribution interrupts the cycle of thinking about yourself and your problems. It puts the focus on others and creates a feel-good experience. There are so many ways to contribute. You can contribute financially or volunteer your time or talents. And if you feel like money and time are tight, know that it doesn't have to be much. It might be $1.00, $10.00, $100.00, or $1,000.00. It might be volunteering for an hour, a day, or a week. Do what works for you, but get in the game of contribution. When we contribute to others, it feels good to them and us. It's a win-win situation. And when we feel good, it causes us to want to contribute even more.

One of the easiest ways to contribute to another person is to acknowledge or appreciate them verbally. There are so many opportunities to do this. My family travels a lot, so there are many people along the way to thank for being helpful, keeping us safe, and providing service. Yes, it may be their job, but it still feels good to be acknowledged for a job well done. Or if there is nothing to thank a person for, you can tell someone that it's nice to see them. My wife frequently tells me, "I'm glad you're here." That feels good and makes me smile every time. It feels good to be seen and appreciated. Are you glad to have certain people in your life? Let them know. There doesn't have to be a special occasion. Become someone who contributes to others, who acknowledges and appreciates others. You can be someone who increases the value of others. **Keep practicing contribution.**

MOVE YOUR BODY

I will not tell you how to exercise or even that you should exercise. But, if it is possible for you to do so, then consider moving your body. Moving your body increases blood flow and oxygenation and releases feel-good hormones. It is an easy and quick way to change your emotional state. Just getting outside for a few minutes can change your whole perspective. It may be walking the dog, riding a bike, swimming, Tai Chi, hiking, running, paddle boarding, playing pickleball, dancing, weight training, etc. This is one of the key elements that can create feel-good emotions. There are lots of ways to do it. **Keep practicing movement.**

CONTENT CONSUMPTION

I will not tell you what content you should or shouldn't consume. But I will remind you that what you focus on, you feel. What you focus on expands and becomes your point of attraction.

I gave up listening to and reading the news years ago. It was one of the best things I did for my mental health. Some people will say, "But we need to stay informed." Yes, I get that. I am a citizen who writes to my representatives and makes my opinion known. However, that doesn't require reading or listening to the news daily. I used to start my day with the news. As a result, I would feel disappointed, discouraged, or upset. Then I would go and share the news I heard with my wife. So I would dump all my disappointment into her morning. This is NOT a feel-good way to start the day. So I gave up the news. The essential topics that interest me still find their way to me. I am informed, but I don't need to have it as a mainstay of my life. I've learned that 98% of the news doesn't affect my daily life. So I will put my energy into places that do affect my life and create a feel-good impact.

Consider the content you are consuming. How much social media do you consume? How do you feel as a result of what you are viewing? If you feel good, great. If you feel jealous, inadequate, or fall into the comparison game, consider the impact of what you are viewing.

I encourage you to consider listening to content that inspires you, lifts you up, enlightens you, promotes growth, and moves you along toward your desired outcomes. There is so much fantastic content out there. Take your pick of the seemingly endless number of books you can read or speakers you can watch and listen to on

YouTube or live settings. **Keep practicing the consumption of feel-good content.**

INCANTATIONS AND AFFIRMATIONS

We've talked about the power of language. It's the primary way we create our world. Some people don't think incantations or affirmations work. I assure you they do. We have been practicing affirmations all of our lives. Most of us have yet to realize it. They frequently sound like this: "I can't do that. I don't have enough experience. Others are doing it better than I am. I'm too shy. I don't have enough money. There's never enough time. Life is a struggle. I don't have what it takes. I'll probably fail. Things like that don't happen to me. I have the worst luck." These aren't just sentences. They are affirmations or incantations that have been turned into programs that hold us back. Our mind is so practiced at saying them or some version of them that we don't even realize it. Yet the consequences are real.

Begin practicing some new and empowering affirmations. I came up with ten over the years and still use them regularly. And by the way, I've said them so many times for so long now that I can't go back to thinking the way I used to think. And that's a good thing! Here you go:

- I am resourceful, capable, and flexible.
- There is always enough time for the things that are important to me.
- Good things are lined up, stacked up, and showing up daily.

- Life is always working out for my greatest growth and evolution.
- I am a frequent recipient of money, gifts, and services.
- I meet the moment with a light heart and navigate the "now" with ease and joy.
- Life is beautiful. Life is a gift.
- All that I need is within me right now.
- Money is constantly in circulation and flowing to me. I am part of the circulation of wealth.
- I live a feel-good life of freedom, fun, and philanthropy.

Feel free to use any of these as they are or wordsmith them to serve you. I would love to hear what you come up with. **Keep practicing feel-good affirmations.**

PLAY

I love playing. We play so many games in our home. It may be a fast-paced game of Boggle, a long and intense game of Catan, cards, board games, bocce ball, pickleball, and four square (yes, even four square!) We love games. They are fun. They promote connection and laughter, create memories, and facilitate inclusion. Many adults stop playing. I get it. Life gets busy, and we fall into other patterns of watching TV or hanging out on our phones. Play gets pushed to the side. But the whole intent of play is to feel good! We make play a priority in our household, which has created many opportunities for rich bonding.

One of the things we did for years was to host an annual evening of talent at our home. We would invite friends and acquaintances to our house one evening in the summer, during which people shared all sorts of talents. It was one of the highlights of our summer. There were instruments, including pianos, cellos, violins, and drums. There were recitations of poetry along with stand-up comedy. People rode unicycles, performed magic, did goofy human tricks, sang songs, and there was lots of good food and connection. Oh, and there were lots and lots of bubbles. I love bubbles, so we always had bubble machines to fill the air with thousands of iridescent spheres of various sizes. Those nights were so much fun. I fondly remember looking out across the yard and seeing 50 people smiling, laughing, and feeling connected. Those nights didn't cost anything, were easy to set up, and people had a wonderful, memorable time. **Keep practicing play.**

INVEST IN MINDSET

Mindset is a fixed set of beliefs, decisions, and attitudes that help us make sense of ourselves and the world around us. People are willing to invest in technology, clothing, entertainment, toys, makeup, etc. But relatively few people are willing to invest in the number one thing that determines the quality of their lives - their mindset!

Mindset determines the quality of our marriages, our friendships, how much we earn, and how much we spend or save. It largely determines how we feel in our bodies. You have likely seen or heard the expression: "Mindset is everything." It's not just a fluffy quote. It really does determine the quality of your life.

My family has invested tens of thousands of dollars in personal development over the years. That sounds crazy to many people. But let me ask you something. How valuable is a sense of fulfillment to you? How valuable is a thriving marriage to you? How valuable is the success of your business? How valuable is your health and fitness? Your beliefs, decisions, and attitudes massively impact all areas of your life. The most significant investment we can make is in our mindset.

This is why I hire coaches. I need a high level of accountability in my life. I need a coach to ask me challenging questions, help me see my blind spots, and help keep me engaged and inspired. When you look at professional sporting teams, they all have coaches. Why? Because the coach can see things from a different perspective. They have a ton of experience and wisdom from which to draw. The best athletes, actors, and salespeople all have coaches. They know there is always that next level, and they need help to get there. They are open to help, feedback, and ongoing growth.

So ask yourself, "Is it time to invest in me?" There are so many opportunities. There are online workshops, live seminars, and a plethora of YouTube videos. Or you can hire a coach. In fact, if you've made it this far in the book, you may be ready to work with me. Reach out and set up a free discovery call with me. We can discover where you may be stuck, stalled, or plateaued. There's no obligation and no pressure. I'll listen to what's happening in your life, ask some questions, and let you know if I can help you. It's that simple. Investing in my mindset allowed me to create the marriage of my dreams, heal relationships in my family, generate significant revenue, make a difference for others, and create an incredibly feel-good life. Visit my website to see what services are available, or reach out to me at fletcher@fletcherellingson.com. Reference "discovery call" in the subject line, and you will receive instructions on scheduling our visit. If you've ever thought about doing something like this but have put it off until "someday," I want you to know that "someday" has arrived. Your life is **now,** so take action. You have nothing to lose and an incredible feel-good life to gain.

I look forward to meeting you, and until then, get out there and be a source of kindness. Be a source of contribution. You do have something to offer this world, and I believe in you.

Oh, and of course.... **KEEP PRACTICING!**

Key Takeaways

- Suffering diminishes our ability to make progress.
- The Practice of Feeling Good is access to progress.
- Our mindset determines the results and the quality of our lives.

Opportunity to Practice

1. Write down three feel-good affirmations that you can begin implementing into your day. You can come up with your own or choose from the list of ten I provided earlier in this chapter.
2. Where do you want to experience more play in your life? Write down two areas and brainstorm ideas for making it happen.
3. Consider the content you consume regularly. Does it feel good and empower you, or disempowering and put you on a track for suffering? Commit to consuming more inspiring and motivating content.
4. Decide right now that feeling good is a high priority and commit to practicing it in your life.

Don't Just Read About Transformation - Experience It in Yourself!

Book your life-changing *"Feel-Good Discovery Session"* now. This strategic one-on-one call is designed to identify exactly where and why you feel stuck or plateaued and open up access to new results.

Experience It in Your Organization

Ignite change within your organization and learn how to create a feel-good work environment that cultivates genuine positivity and greater productivity. Inquire about Fletcher's availability for speaking engagements, workshops, or consulting.

VISIT: www.FletcherEllingson.com

ACKNOWLEDGMENTS

I have been a student of personal development for most of my life. It began when I was in elementary school. I know that may seem like an early age to begin thinking about mindset, but we had the privilege of having an inspirational speaker, Wayne Bredberg, present to us one afternoon in the gymnasium. I'm sure Wayne had many outstanding messages that day, but two stuck with me for the rest of my life. The first was to start your day with PMA (Positive Mental Attitude), and the second was to expect something wonderful to happen! Both statements were on a reflective sticker on my metal bed frame. I saw that message every single day for years.

Since those early years, so many people have helped shape my thinking. Thank you to all of my mentors and coaches, including Tony Robbins, David Bayer, Esther Hicks, Darcy Bailey, Michelle Cooper, Peter Hill, JB Glossinger, T.J. Hoisington, and the leaders at Landmark Education. This book and my current experience of life are possible because of the teachings and inspiration of those mentioned. And there are a host of other wonderful servants who modeled living life to the fullest who I've never personally met but who have influenced and inspired me: Zig Ziglar, Les Brown, Brene Brown, Oprah Winfrey, Joel Osteen, and Bob Proctor.

I also extend my gratitude to my mother, Eleanor Ellingson, for always supporting me and powerfully modeling kindness. My father, Gary Ellingson, for modeling entrepreneurship and strength. My step-father, Allen Matson, for modeling hard work and service. Our six children, Naomi, Sophia, Oliver, Cara, Camille, and Kayla, for always being up for play, conversation, and growth. My wonderful in-laws Les, Virginia, Van, and Jackie, for their incredible generosity and willingness to wholeheartedly welcome me into their family. Thank you to my friends for frequently reminding me of who I am and what I am capable of creating. Thank you to my clients for trusting me, inspiring me, and evolving with me. Thank you, Maui, for your magic and inspiration in my life. And finally, thank you, Amy, for being the most wonderful co-creator of this feel-good life.

ABOUT FLETCHER ELLINGSON

Fletcher Ellingson is a speaker, coach, author, and creator of The Practice of Feeling Good in Business and Life. He helps his clients break free from financial struggle, overwhelm, and persistent worry so they can spend more time doing what they love, contribute to their families, and impact their communities.

Fletcher has helped hundreds of entrepreneurs and successful professionals embrace the principles of The Practice of Feeling Good. As a result, they've radically shifted their thinking and produced outstanding outcomes in their health, wealth, and relationships. His clients learn to create and navigate life with greater ease and joy using a combination of science, psychology, and inquiry into being.

Fletcher has studied with some of the best minds in the personal development industry. In addition to over 25 years of speaking for audiences across the United States, he regularly contributes to a newspaper column and hosts a local TV show that addresses topics of health, wealth, and relationships.

WHAT FLETCHER'S CLIENTS ARE SAYING...

"One of the most talented individuals I have encountered in terms of creatively addressing challenges and re-envisioning what is possible is Fletcher Ellingson."

- Rufus Woods, Publisher Emeritus of The Wenatchee World

"Fletcher helped grow our company from a $200K a year company to a multi-million dollar a year company. As a result of implementing the principles and tools in his courses, our company more than 10x its revenues. My advice: Sign up, listen up, and implement his program ASAP."

- Chris R., Owner of SunGraphic.com

"Our management teams from all three offices had an amazing night attending our leadership training - The Practice of Feeling Good in Business & Life, presented by Fletcher Ellingson! Fletcher is the real deal! He gave our management team a toolbox full of new ways to lead - and gave me a new appreciation for leadership training!

If you haven't looked into a leadership coach, please reach out to him for details - it's well worth the investment for you, your team, and your business!"

- Edwin E., Owner of iPro Building Services

"Before Fletcher's course, I was making progress in business, but I felt stressed, spread thin, and anxious that if I didn't keep at it, I would lose all I had worked for. At the same time, I wasn't feeling connected to my friends, family, or even myself. Fletcher helped me see success doesn't have to come at the expense of personal fulfillment. My business has expanded in ways I didn't believe possible without sacrificing my relationships. I have so much more confidence in myself. I now have the tools to stay positive, hopeful, energized, effective, confident, connected, and most of all, I recognize it's my decision… and no circumstance can take that away from me."

- Sydney G., Co-Owner, KW Real Estate NCW

"Every once in a while, you come across an individual who has characteristics that are so dynamic that you're simply drawn to them as a person. Fletcher Ellingson is one of those people – positivity, strong work ethic, and a never give up attitude. He goes beyond what we commonly think of as a life coach; he is a motivator, an accountability coach, an inspirational guide through the journey of life."

- Kory K., High School Principal

"Fletcher challenged me to recognize my own potential for bringing success, prosperity, and peace into my life. My self-image improved, my relationships became stronger and more meaningful, and my anxiety and stress greatly diminished. Fletcher helped me understand how I was stopping myself from accessing the life I really wanted to manifest. Once I learned what was preventing me from mastering my destiny, I knew what to do to reach my full potential. I am on my way to the life I desire and deserve!"

- Kim S., Real Estate Entrepreneur

Made in United States
Troutdale, OR
08/15/2023